CRESCENT CITY

SILVER

Published by

THE HISTORIC NEW ORLEANS COLLECTION
THE KEMPER AND LEILA WILLIAMS FOUNDATION
533 Royal Street   New Orleans

SILVER

an exhibition of nineteenth-century
New Orleans silver

THE HISTORIC NEW ORLEANS COLLECTION
NEW ORLEANS, LOUISIANA
April 16, 1980 - September 13, 1980

ANGLO-AMERICAN ART MUSEUM
LOUISIANA STATE UNIVERSITY
BATON ROUGE, LOUISIANA
September 21, 1980 - November 21, 1980

Cover illustration:
Pitcher   ca. 1852-1853
Made by Küchler & Himmel
Retailed by Hyde & Goodrich
Cat. no. 36

Drawing by Sam Still

CONTENTS

FOREWORD

By very happy coincidence The Historic New Orleans Collection occupies what was once the site of one of the earliest silversmiths in the Crescent City. This smithy, unfortunately, was destroyed by the great fire of 1788; but the art of working in silver happily survived, and continued to flourish in New Orleans until the beginning of the twentieth century.

Our study of the collection's own silver holdings disclosed how very scarce was the information available on New Orleans silver. Our curatorial department expressed concern over the lack of primary and secondary documentation on the subject. At or about the very time when our staff was concerning itself with the topic of New Orleans silver, we were approached by Carey T. Mackie, H. Parrott Bacot, and Charles L. Mackie, each of whom had deeply interested himself in the subject, and who had been conducting extensive research into the history of New Orleans silver. Their work included very diligent efforts to locate as many examples as possible of silver locally made and locally sold. These enthusiasts were combining their material, and they had come to the conclusion that a properly mounted exhibit, with an elegantly presented catalogue, not only would arouse great public interest, but also would serve to introduce the topic of New Orleans silver to students as an area for serious investigation. This project thus became a reality, as the joint effort of our own staff and of Mr. Bacot and the Mackies.

The nucleus of the exhibit is the outstanding silver which has been lent to us by the Anglo-American Art Museum, Louisiana State University, to which have been added very fine pieces from our own collection. Choice items have been lent by public institutions and by private individuals. We hope that, as a local museum, our featuring New Orleans silver will bring those who own it further to appreciate, to protect, and to cherish their silver for the enjoyment of future generations. Finally, as a research center, The Historic New Orleans Collection, in publishing its first major catalogue on the subject, *Crescent City Silver*, hopes that this will be the first reference tool of its kind in a long series of reference works which the subject so richly deserves.

Stanton Frazar
January, 1980

ACKNOWLEDGMENTS

The organization of this exhibition and the production of this catalogue consumed the efforts, energy, help, and enthusiasm of many, many people. We should specially like to thank the curatorial department of The Historic New Orleans Collection for their essential and invaluable participation. Dode Platou, Chief Curator; John A Mahé II, Curator; Rosanne McCaffrey, Associate Curator; John H. Lawrence, Assistant Curator; and Lisette C. Oser, Registrar, all made the labor of assembling this material more pleasant. Staff members Carolyn Dong, Florence Jumonville, Catherine C. Kahn, and Gertrude Magnuson provided assistance. Also, our indebtedness to Stanton Frazar, Director of The Historic New Orleans Collection, for making possible the exhibit and this catalogue is great.

Under the direction of Oscar G. Richard III, and through the patronage of Friends of the Museum, the Anglo-American Art Museum at Louisiana State University, Baton Rouge, contributed significantly. And the expertise of Christopher A. Hentz, Assistant Professor of Fine Arts, and his students, Ellis Joubert and Thomas Lorio, was called upon to repair and refurbish a number of silver pieces.

Unquestionably, others have aided in the research and the documentation of New Orleans silver. To the following we gratefully acknowledge our appreciation: James H. Adams, Jr.; Jay P. Altmayer; Pamela Bardo; Mrs. Beauregard L. Bassich; David B. Warren, Associate Director of Bayou Bend Collection; Mrs. H. Payne Breazeale, Sr.; Mrs. Jack C. Brier; Ricky Brocato; Mrs. Thomas M. Logan Bruns; Powell Casey; Mr. and Mrs. William K. Christovich; Dr. and Mrs. A. Brooks Cronan, Jr.; Boyd Cruise; Mr. and Mrs. Louis Cusachs; David R. Dugas; Thea Engelhard; Mrs. Albert B. Fay; Mary O'Neill Victor, Director of the Fine Arts Museum of the South at Mobile; Alice Forsyth; Katharine Logan Forsyth; Mrs. William B. Forsyth; Mr. and Mrs. Sam H. Fowlkes; Mrs. H. Bennett Fox; James V. Gillespie; Edmund J. Glenny; Morton M. Goldberg; Mrs. John B. Gooch; Mrs. Frances Grabe; Barry A. Greenlaw; the late Philip H. Hammerslough; Nathan Halpern, Jr.; Edith Haupt; Betty Hertzog; Virginia Holbrook; Dr. and Mrs. Jack D. Holden; Sue Kerr Hyams; Margaret Rose Ingate; Bessie Jones; Rose Kahn; Emile N. Kuntz; Mr. and Mrs. Waldo P. Lambdin; Mrs. Robert Layton, Sr.; Paul Leaman, Jr.; J. Thomas Lewis; Rose Lambert, Librarian of the Louisiana State Museum; Mr. and Mrs. Harry McCall, Jr.; Justine G. McCarthy; Mr. and Mrs. John F. McCoy; Mrs. Robert Martinez; Mr. and Mrs. C. Layton Merritt; E. John Bullard, Director, Charles Mo, Registrar, and Jeannette Downing, Librarian, of the New Orleans Museum of Art; James B. Norris; Carol Layton Parsons; V. A. Patterson; Gordon N. Simons of the Pensacola Historical Museum; Mrs. A. Fred Renaud, Jr.; Sally K. Evans Reeves; Jennie E. Robicheaux; Darla Rushing; Nadine Russell; Mr. and Mrs. Raymond J. St. Germain; the late Harold Schilke; Mrs. Joseph V. Schlosser; Dorothy Sires; Anne M. R. Strachan; Kenneth T. Urquhart; Ernest C. Villeré; Burton G. Tremaine, Director, and Phillip M. Johnston, Chief Curator and Curator of Decorative Arts of the Wadsworth Atheneum; Mr. and Mrs. Peter B. Waters; Mrs. Edmund Wingfield; Nancy Richards and Deborah Waters of the Henry Francis duPont Winterthur Museum; the Reverend Charles Wood of the Episcopal Student Center at the Louisiana State University; Alan Shestack, Director, Patricia Kane, Director of American Decorative Arts, and Gerald W. R. Ward of Yale University Art Gallery; Mr. and Mrs. Robert E. Young.

Carey T. Mackie
H. Parrott Bacot
Charles L. Mackie

The *CRESCENT CITY SILVER* exhibition presents for comparison examples of silver from the three intermingling traditions in New Orleans: French, American, and German. Each group made contributions to the developing styles of local silver, which were influenced in turn by the lifestyle of the city itself. The immigrant French silversmiths, in their shops in the French Quarter of the city, made plain, heavy, solid flatware; and they imported or brought back with them from their visits to France, silver baskets, bowls, tureens, and other fancy items in the latest French styles. The silversmiths from the northeastern United States introduced, from their shops on or near Canal Street, the silver patterns so popular on the east coast, modified to suit the French tastes of the city. Many trained immigrant German craftsmen enriched the surfaces of silver hollowware with chased and engraved details in a variety of designs and decorative motifs. The objects selected for exhibit and illustrated in the catalogue are representative of the finest silver products made by these groups for the large local market. The assembling of so large a group of extant pieces should now stimulate further research into the field of New Orleans silver.

The INTRODUCTION that follows provides a brief view of the migration of silversmiths to New Orleans from Europe and of the influx from other parts of the United States. The BIOGRAPHY that precedes the examples of each smith's works is the first compilation of the lives of the artisans and merchants heretofore overlooked. It is hoped that more primary material will surface to document further the firms and their workers.

The CATALOGUE ENTRIES are divided into two groups. Part I begins with Hyde & Goodrich, a company which subsequently changed names and partnerships several times, and continued into the twentieth century as the foremost supplier of silver in the lower Mississippi Valley. Part II groups together in chronological order all the other silversmiths represented in the exhibition.

The LIST OF NEW ORLEANS SILVERSMITHS includes not only all who identified themselves as silversmiths but also all other artisans who, though listed in some other trade, produced silver. The list, along with the photographs in the NEW ORLEANS MAKERS' MARKS, can encourage collectors and owners of old silver to learn more about their pieces and to bring them to the attention of researchers in the field.

The economic situation in the silver and gold markets has lately tended to overshadow the historical value of the objects made with these metals. The exhibition and catalogue *CRESCENT CITY SILVER* hopefully will reemphasize collecting and protecting as important factors for those who possess, inherit, or buy New Orleans silver.

John A. Mahé II
Catalogue and Exhibition Coordinator

INTRODUCTION

With few exceptions, the Louisiana silversmiths of the colonial eighteenth century were French or of French extraction. The silver articles which they created were similar to contemporary styles in France, but little of the locally produced silver has survived. Also rare today is the foreign silver imported from France, Spain, and England to supplement the local supply. Various reasons account for the scarcity of all silver of the period: it was difficult for the local smiths to obtain raw materials; the expense of manufacturing the pieces made silver a great luxury in eighteenth-century Louisiana; and New Orleans was still a small town with few inhabitants able to afford such indulgences. The fires of 1788 and 1794 which razed a large part of the city, burned the silver workshops, stores, as well as private homes and their contents. Another probable cause of the scarcity of silver of the 1700s was the practice of melting down older pieces to accommodate changing tastes or to replace silver items badly worn through hard use.

Most known surviving New Orleans silver dates from the nineteenth century. Manufacturers and retailers of this period fall into three groups: French, American (from the Eastern seaboard), and German. The nineteenth-century French silversmiths continued to produce silverware in the style of the late eighteenth-century French pieces. P. Bertin, Louis Couvertié, Jean Delarue, Pierre Lamothe, Jean-Marie Lamothe, and Jean-Baptiste Lamothe were French silversmiths who arrived in New Orleans in the first quarter of the century. Another Frenchman, who appeared later, was Casimir Rouyer, a silver plater known to have imported great quantities of finished goods from France.

As a result of political disturbances at home, Germans immigrated to New Orleans during the late 1840s and early 1850s. Included in this group were silversmiths Adolphe Himmel, Christopf Christian Küchler, Joseph Rafel, Maurice Scooler, and Bernard Terfloth. P. Zimmermann and Charles H. Zimmermann came in the 1860s; Henry and Theresa Hausmann arrived in the early 1870s.

Practicing silversmiths coming from the major Eastern American cities overlap the other two groups both chronologically and stylistically. American smiths began settling in New Orleans around the turn of the nineteenth century. It was not until 1815, when the battle assured that New Orleans would remain an American city, that the major wave of Americans came. These vigilant entrepreneurs not only sold pieces in the east coast styles, but also catered to the substantial market for articles in the French taste. Early pieces marked by American manufacturers and retailers were indistinguishable from popular French styles produced by the local Franco-American silversmiths. It was also common practice for Americans to employ German immigrant craftsmen. Much of the finest New Orleans silver made in the era preceding the Civil War was actually fashioned by Germans for sale by the American retailers.

The Americans included: H.E. Baldwin & Co.; Bliss & Whittemore; S. & B. Brower; H.P. Buckley; Gregor & Wilson; A.B. Griswold & Co.; Henry Harland; Harland & Blair; Henderson & Gaines; Hyde & Goodrich; E.A. Tyler; Whittemore & Blair; James A. Young; and Anthony Rasch. Rasch was a native of Germany, but had lived and worked in Philadelphia before coming to New Orleans, and thus is grouped with the Americans.

The interruption of the Civil War and then the proliferation of less expensive, machine-produced silver from the North gradually brought about the decline of locally manufactured silver. New Orleans silversmiths could not compete with large silver manufacturing firms such as Gorham in Providence; Tiffany and Company in New York; J. E. Caldwell of Philadelphia; and Samuel Kirk and Company of Baltimore. By the late 1870s, silversmithing in New Orleans had become a moribund craft. There was a brief revival in the last decade of the nineteenth century, but this new enthusiasm barely survived past 1900.

Carey T. Mackie
H. Parrott Bacot
Charles L. Mackie

CATALOGUE

Researched and compiled by
Carey T. Mackie
H. Parrott Bacot
Charles L. Mackie

Edited by

Rosanne McCaffrey
Dode Platou
John H. Lawrence
John A. Mahé II

ABBREVIATIONS

H. = height
W. = extreme width
L. = length
D. = diameter
WT. = weight
gm = grams
oz = ounces
cm = centimeters
in = inches
dwt = pennyweight

CONVERSIONS

1 in = 2.54 cm
1 troy oz = 31.103 gm
20 dwt = 1 troy oz

PART I

JAMES NEVINS HYDE

James Nevins Hyde was born January 24, 1788, at Norwich, Connecticut, the son of Captain James Hyde and his wife, Martha Nevins Hyde, of Bean Hill, Norwich.

James N. Hyde first appears in New York City directories in 1810. He is included as a jeweler in 1812, and is listed as working out of the same location as Rufus Lewis Nevins, his first cousin, in 1815. It is highly unlikely that the partnership of Hyde & Nevins was operating as early as 1798, but seems to date from about 1815. Rufus Lewis Nevins was the son of Captain David Nevins and his wife, Mary Hubbard Nevins. He withdrew from the partnership in 1819 to become a Wall Street stock and exchange broker.

James N. Hyde continued to operate a jewelry business both in New York and New Orleans. Sometime in 1829, he formed the Hyde & Goodrich partnership in New Orleans with his brother-in-law, Charles Whiting Goodrich. Hyde withdrew from Hyde & Goodrich on January 7, 1837, and died in New Orleans from yellow fever on September 24, 1838. He was buried in the Girod Street Cemetery, New Orleans.

In all probability, James Nevins Hyde was the only partner of Hyde & Goodrich who was a silversmith. His ability appears to have been limited to spectacles and spoons. While in partnership with Nevins, he is known to have retailed hollowware by William B. Heyer of New York.

1. **Spectacles   ca. 1812-1835**

MARK (on right bow at hinge): "HYDE" in rectangle.

DESCRIPTION: Oval, silver frames enclosing glass, joined by wide nosepiece; hinged, extending temples.

MEASUREMENTS: L. extended 15.0 cm (5⅞ in); W. 12.0 cm (4⅞ in); WT. 15.6 gm (.50 oz)

LOAN: *Private Collection*

Silver spectacle frames were in common use during the first half of the nineteenth century. Several portraits show Louisianians wearing this popular type. The frames were fitted on each side with movable temples that extended back over the ears, and easily adjusted to fit all sizes of heads.

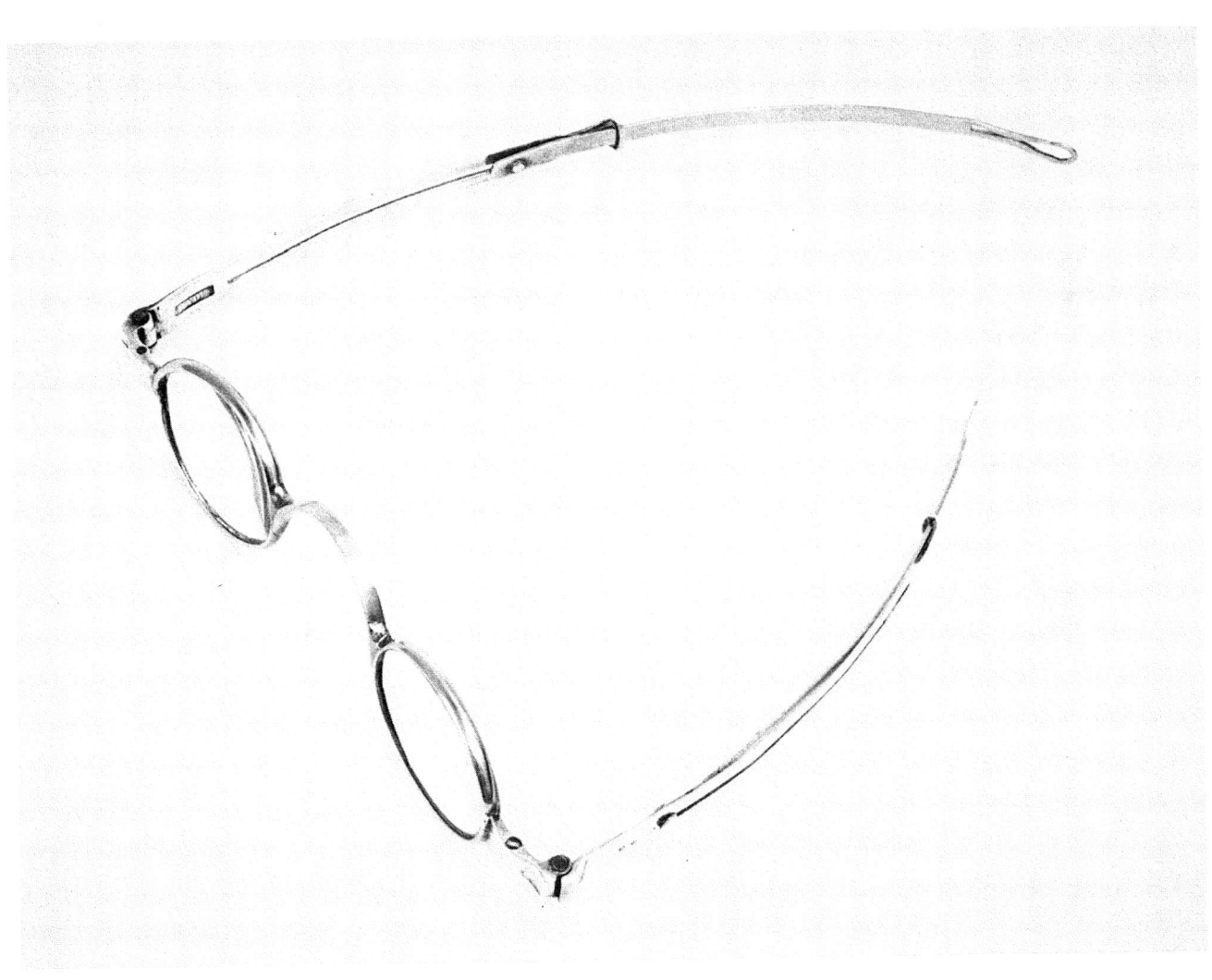

HYDE & GOODRICH,

THE LARGEST IMPORTERS OF
JEWELRY, WATCHES, PLATED-WARE, GUNS AND PISTOLS.
AND THE ONLY MANUFACTURERS OF
GOLD AND SILVER WARE,
IN THE SOUTH--WEST.

Corner of Canal and Royal streets, New Orleans.
This House has been established forty years in New Orleans.

Hyde & Goodrich advertisement. *New Orleans Merchants' Diary and Guide, 1857 and 1858.* New Orleans: E.C. Wharton, printer, 1857. (The Historic New Orleans Collection)

HYDE & GOODRICH

The original partnership between Messrs. Hyde and Goodrich was created in 1829, as a continuation under a new name of the New Orleans branch of James N. Hyde & Co., of New York. James N. Hyde & Co., of New York was the successor of Hyde & Nevins, New York, manufacturers and jewelry retailers. Hyde & Nevins was founded by James Nevins Hyde and his first cousin, Rufus Lewis Nevins, in 1815.

James N. Hyde was most probably a working silversmith. He may even have learned his craft from one of his two first cousins: William Cleveland (1770-1837), or Aaron Porter Cleveland (1782-184?), both important Connecticut silversmiths.

In 1816 or 1817, Hyde & Nevins expanded their operations to New Orleans under the name of James N. Hyde & Co. In 1818, Charles Whiting Goodrich and Samuel Goodrich, brothers-in-law of James N. Hyde, together with their families moved from New York City to New Orleans. A year later C.W. Goodrich was appointed agent for Hyde & Co., and ran the business during Hyde's long sojourns to New York. C.W. Goodrich was almost certainly not a silversmith although like his brother-in-law, he was related to several prominent Connecticut craftsmen. Among Goodrich's silversmith relatives were: his grandfather, Charles Whiting (1725-1765); his great uncles, William

Bradford Whiting (1731-1796), and Ebenezer Whiting (1735-1794); his uncle, Charles Bradford Whiting (1751-after 1790); his cousin, Samuel Noyes (1747-1781); and, by the marriage of his and James N. Hyde's cousin, Abigail Leffingwell Hyde, Henry Harland (1789-1841).

Hyde & Goodrich was a succession of partnerships including at various times: James N. Hyde, who withdrew in 1837, and died in New Orleans from yellow fever in 1838; Charles Whiting Goodrich, who died in 1849; Edward Goodrich Hyde, son of James Nevins Hyde, who withdrew in 1861; William McLeary Goodrich, son of Charles Whiting Goodrich; Henry Thomas, Jr., brother-in-law of the younger Mr. Hyde, admitted before 1843; and, Arthur Breese Griswold, brother-in-law of the younger Mr. Goodrich, admitted to the partnership by 1854.

The bombardment of Fort Sumter by the Confederates on April 14, 1861, brought about the dissolution of the firm. Shortly after the distant rumblings of war reached Edward G. Hyde, he notified the partnership that he was withdrawing. Under a Louisiana law of 1857 the partnership could not continue to carry the name of Hyde in the firm's title.

The actual management of Hyde & Goodrich had been left to Henry Thomas, Jr., and A. B.

Griswold. Even William M. Goodrich was not participating to the extent he had earlier. By 1861, Goodrich was fifty-six years old and rapidly losing interest in the day-to-day affairs of the business. The new partnership, succeeding Hyde & Goodrich, was formed under the name of Thomas, Griswold & Co. with the remaining partners, Henry Thomas, Jr., A.B. Griswold, and William M. Goodrich. Henry Ginder and A. L. Abbott had small interests.

Unsettled times and the immediate effect of the Civil War on New Orleans prevented the firm from changing the Hyde & Goodrich sign on the building. In fact, the name change to Thomas, Griswold & Co. may have gone completely unnoticed by the bulk of the local population.

The death of Henry Thomas, Jr. before the end of the war required the further change of name of the partnership to A.B. Griswold & Co., in 1865.

During the early years of the partnership, Hyde & Goodrich sold silver manufactured by New England firms. Specific early pieces in the popular French styles may indicate that some locally-made silver may have been sold through Hyde & Goodrich. However, many pieces appearing to be French in construction and detail were actually manufactured in the eastern United States for sale in the New Orleans area.

During the early 1850s, with the increased demand and the fortuitous influx to New Orleans of highly-skilled German craftsmen, Hyde & Goodrich sold locally-made silver. Most notably, the short-lived partnership of Küchler & Himmel produced magnificent Rococo-revival pieces. Later the store was kept well-stocked by the individual efforts of the former partners working independently. Eventually, Adolphe Himmel was employed to produce silver exclusively for Hyde & Goodrich. Although the firm's stock was supplemented with works of other manufacturers, Himmel continued to be *major-domo* of silver production through the successive partnerships until about 1869.

Hyde & Goodrich store, corner of Canal and Royal Streets. "Touro Buildings," undated lithograph by Hammond. (The Historic New Orleans Collection 1954.9.1)

2. Beaker ca. 1845

MARK (on bottom): "HYDE & GOODRICH" in rectangle.

DESCRIPTION: Round body; straight, seamed sides tapered from flared lip with applied molding to baseband with applied molding and beading. "J.W.B./Agr. Socy./1845" engraved in script on body.

MEASUREMENTS: H. 8.3 cm (3¼ in); D. lip 7.3 cm (2⅞ in); D. base 6.0 cm (2⅜ in); WT. 76.9 gm (2.47 oz)

PROVENANCE: J. W. Bell.

LOAN: *Mr. Harry McCall, Jr.*
New Orleans, Louisiana

3. Beaker ca. 1845-1861

MARK (on bottom): "HYDE & GOODRICH" in rectangle.

DESCRIPTION: Round body with tapered, seamed sides; band with applied molding and beading at lip and base; signs of engine turning on base. "M.S.P." engraved in script on side of body.

MEASUREMENTS: H. 8.3 cm (3¼ in); D. lip 7.5 cm (2¹⁵⁄₁₆ in); D. base 6.7 cm (2⁹⁄₁₆ in); WT. 115.3 gm (3.71 oz)

Anglo-American Art Museum   77.12
Louisiana State University
Baton Rouge, Louisiana

4. Teaspoon Cup   ca. 1845-1855

MARK (on bottom of bowl): "HYDE & GOODRICH" in rectangle.

DESCRIPTION: Rococo-revival pear-shaped goblet on high splayed foot with applied molding; applied beaded band below flared lip and on foot; body decorated with repoussé and chased marshland duck hunting scene and with reserve of flowers and leaves; chased wave band encircles bowl at juncture with base. "J.E.U." engraved in script in cartouche.

MEASUREMENTS: H. 16.4 cm (6 ⁷/₁₆ in); D. lip 9.5 cm (3³/₄ in); D. base 8.2 cm (3¹/₂ in); WT. 192.8 gm (6.20 oz)

PROVENANCE: The initials "J.E.U." are those of the second Mrs. Benjamin Morgan Harrod: Jane Eugenia Uhlhorn, daughter of Dr. Charles L. Uhlhorn. She died October 4, 1917.

LOAN: *New Orleans Museum of Art   (H) 14.41*
New Orleans, Louisiana
Gift of Mrs. Eugenia U. Harrod

Changing lifestyles and customs of the nineteenth century reflected a decline in the use of once popular silver items, such as tankards and porringers, and the introduction of a great variety of new objects. With increased prosperity throughout America, one article almost anyone could afford was a silver teaspoon. Perhaps it was the abundance of these spoons that brought about the spoon holder, or teaspoon cup, as it was referred to by the ancestors of Mrs. Eugenia U. Harrod. Teaspoon cups were usually glass or ceramic, and a silver one is an unusual form. Also unusual, at such an early date, is the decoration with a popular local sporting scene.

5. Waiter ca. 1845-1850

MARKS (on bottom): "HYDE & GOODRICH" in rectangle; "W & H" in oval, partially rubbed.

DESCRIPTION: Flat, circular body; raised rim with shaped edge of "C"-scrolls, waves, and shells; raised on three scroll supports. Laurel wreath engraved in center.

MEASUREMENTS: H. 2.5 cm (1 in); D. 20.9 cm (8¼ in); WT. 337.7 gm (10.86 oz)

LOAN: *Private Collection*

The New York firm of Wood & Hughes, a successor to Gale, Wood & Hughes, was one of the first large-scale manufacturers and wholesalers. It supplied the finished goods for several New Orleans retailers. Numerous surviving pieces of Wood & Hughes flatware and hollowware bear the Hyde & Goodrich mark as retailer. This waiter, or round tray, is the earliest known example with both the Wood & Hughes and the Hyde & Goodrich marks.

The chased border of "C"-scrolls, waves, and shells matches the border on a Hyde & Goodrich cup (cat. no. 6). The ornamentation on both is limited to only the borders, with the bodies remaining unadorned. Later, in the 1850s and 1860s, the same motifs cover almost all the surfaces of goblets, pitchers, and trays, reflecting the Rococo-revival style then popular in hollowware decoration in New Orleans.

6. Two-Handled Cup ca. 1845-1850

MARK (on bottom): "HYDE & GOODRICH" in rectangle.

DESCRIPTION: Round two-handled cup of slightly bulbous shape on flared foot with applied molding and beaded band near juncture with body; applied "C"-scroll, wave, and shell border at lip; scroll handles with flower heads and "C"-scrolls. "James Wilson Lea" engraved in script on side of body; added at later date.

MEASUREMENTS: H. 9.0 cm (3⁹/₁₆ in); D. lip 8.4 cm (3 ⁵/₁₆ in); D. base 5.8 cm (2⁵/₁₆ in); W. 9.7 cm (5¹³/₁₆ in); WT. 196.8 gm (6.33 oz)

LOAN: *Private Collection*

7. Goblet   ca. 1840-1850

MARK (on bottom of bowl):   "HYDE & GOODRICH" in rectangle.

DESCRIPTION: Deep ovoid-shaped bowl; lip with applied molding and beading; trumpet-shaped base with applied vertical foot with beading. Engraved picturesque lake scene with sailboats, lighthouse, and mountain in background, all within engraved floral and foliate cartouche. "John L. Lewis" engraved in script on body opposite cartouche.

MEASUREMENTS: H. 13.4 cm (5$\frac{1}{2}$ in); D. lip 7.2 cm (2 $\frac{13}{16}$ in); D. base 7.0 cm (2$\frac{3}{4}$ in); WT. 121.0 gm (3.89 oz)

PROVENANCE: John L. Lewis was mayor of New Orleans, 1854-1856.

LOAN: *Mr. J. Thomas Lewis*
New Orleans, Louisiana

The earliest sources of silver retailed by Hyde & Goodrich were the manufacturers in New York and Boston. This goblet, marked only "HYDE AND GOODRICH," probably predates the arrival of the firm's own master silversmiths. The shallow engraving of the scenic view on its side bears particular comparison with engraved work done in the northeastern United States.

8. Beaker   ca. 1853-1861

MARKS (on bottom): "HYDE & GOODRICH" incised in arc, above; "MANUFACTURERS" incised, above; "NEW ORLEANS" incised in complementary arc.

DESCRIPTION: Cylindrical body with applied double molding at lip, convex above concave; lower part of cup with double convex moldings; applied band at base with running water-leaf-in-open-heart border against striated ground. "G" engraved in Gothic-revival script, below; crest: out of a ducal coronet, a bull's head.

MEASUREMENTS: H. 9.5 cm (3³⁄₄ in); D. lip 7.9 cm (3¹⁄₈ in); D. base 7.1 cm (2¹³⁄₁₆ in); WT. 148.5 gm (4.77 oz)

Anglo-American Art Museum   80.2.1
Louisiana State University
Baton Rouge, Louisiana
Gift of Dr. and Mrs. A. Brooks Cronan, Jr.

Drinking vessels of various shapes were manufactured in silver during the nineteenth century. Most were intended for only limited use as containers and were presented as gifts on special occasions, or in gratitude for a service rendered. Among the common forms to survive are: the BEAKER (cat. no. 8), with a straight-sided body and no handle; the GOBLET (cat. no. 9), with a deep bell-shaped body on a stemmed base; the CUP (cat. nos. 10-12), with a bowl-shaped body and one handle.

Many vessels were engraved with initials, names, or inscriptions recording the occasion of the gift. Decorative embellishments on the sides were designed to create empty reserves in which the writing could be engraved. The elaborate Rococo-revival style ornamentation covered the rest of the surfaces with waves, scrolls, flowers, and leaves (cat. nos. 6, 10, 4, 9, respectively).

9. Goblet   ca. 1850-1855

MARK (on bottom of bowl): "HYDE & GOODRICH" in rectangle.

DESCRIPTION: Deep, bell-shaped bowl on high, stepped base; Rococo-revival repoussé grapevines, leaves, and clusters of grapes covering body and forming reserve on one side; scalloped grapevine border at lip; raised ring on shaft with grapevine motif against punchwork ground; top of base ornamented with encircling grapevine, leaves, and grape clusters; applied vertical foot.

MEASUREMENTS: H. 20.3 cm (8¹/₁₆ in); D. lip 10.4 cm (4¹/₄ in); D. base 9.0 cm (3⁹/₁₆ in); WT. 295.5 gm (9.50 oz)

Anglo-American Art Museum   80.2.2
Louisiana State University
Baton Rouge, Louisiana
Gift of Dr. and Mrs. A. Brooks Cronan, Jr.

10. Cup   ca. 1850

MARKS (on bottom):   "HYDE & GOODRICH" incised in arc, above; "NEW ORLEANS" incised in complementary arc.

DESCRIPTION: Cylindrical body; molded lip with beading; double-row convex molding above applied vertical foot of diaper banding; repoussé and chased scrolling foliage and flowers forming reserve; simple scroll handle with thumbpiece.

MEASUREMENTS: H. 9.4 cm (3¹¹/₁₆ in); D. lip 7.0 cm (2³/₄ in); D. base 7.2 cm (2¹³/₁₆ in); W. 10.6 cm (4³/₁₆ in); WT. 105.2 gm (3.38 oz)

The Historic New Orleans Collection   1978.175.20
New Orleans, Louisiana

11. Cup   ca. 1850

MARKS (on bottom):   "HYDE & GOODRICH" in rectangle, above; small fleur-de-lis punch.

DESCRIPTION: Slightly bulbous-shaped body; applied beading just below flared lip and on applied splayed foot; repoussé and chased floral sprays and "C"-scrolls on either side of Rococo-revival scroll cartouche; double scroll handle with thumbpiece.

MEASUREMENTS: H. 9.9 cm (3⁷/₈ in); D. lip 7.7 cm (3¹/₈ in); D. base 5.7 cm (2¹/₄ in); W. 11.4 cm (4¹/₂ in); WT. 124.9 gm (4.02 oz)

The Historic New Orleans Collection   1978.175.16
New Orleans, Louisiana

12. Cup   ca. 1850

MARKS (on bottom):   "HYDE & GOODRICH" incised in arc, above; "NEW ORLEANS" incised in complementary arc, partially rubbed.

DESCRIPTION: Round, bulbous-shaped body; flared lip with beading below; running anthemion-in-open-heart band on applied flared foot; repoussé and chased flowers and leaves on either side of Rococo-revival shield-shaped reserve of waves and punchwork; double scroll handle with thumbpiece. "JWW" engraved in script in cartouche.

MEASUREMENTS: H. 9.4 cm (3¹¹/₁₆ in); D. lip 7.8 cm (3 ¹/₁₆ in); D. base 5.7 cm (2¹/₂ in); W. 11.2 cm (4³/₈ in); WT. 134.5 gm (4.32 oz)

The Historic New Orleans Collection   1978.175.14
New Orleans, Louisiana

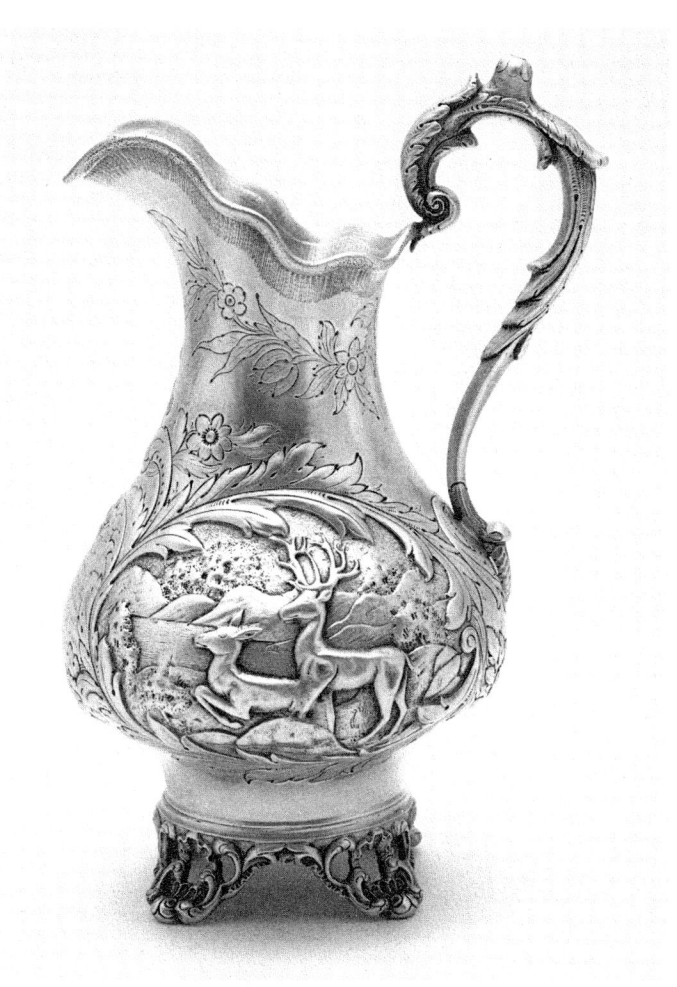

13. Pitcher   ca. 1851

MARK (on bottom of bowl): "HYDE & GOODRICH" in rectangle.

DESCRIPTION: Pear-shaped body; repoussé and chased flowers and scrolling foliage encircling cartouche and two picturesque landscapes, one with dog, other with two deer; chased drapery border below scalloped, molded lip; molded base raised on four high, splayed, pierced scroll feet; leaf-capped scroll handle. "We the undersigned passengers of/the United States Mail Steamship Ohio/tender our regards to Lieut. J. Findly Schench/& beg of him his acceptance of this small /testimonial from his friends. Oct. 5th 1851./C. Stoddard. G. R. Hoyt. L. H. Sandford. J. U. Hunt./G. M. Tollen. M. Bowditch. D. U. Corwin. C. Wheeler./C. Forbes. T. W. Ferren. S. Blunt. I. D. Constock./C. Floyd. F. Catherwood./J. S. Robb. J. L. Pierpont." engraved in cartouche, on body below spout.

MEASUREMENTS: H. 28.7 cm (11⁵/₁₆ in); W. 18.6 cm (7³/₈ in); WT.953.9 gm (30.67 oz)

PROVENANCE: Sotheby Parke Bernet, Inc., New York; Sale 4211, item 43; January 31, 1979.

LOAN: *Mr. Paul Leaman*
       New Orleans, Louisiana

14. Coffee Pot   ca. 1850-1860

MARKS (on bottom): "HYDE & GOODRICH" incised in
arc, above; "NEW ORLEANS" incised in complementary arc.

DESCRIPTION: Pear-shaped body on applied molded circular foot; repoussé and chased shell, wave, and,
"C"-scroll cartouche on each side; chased drapery
border below molded lip with guilloche banding; low
domed lid with cast-flower finial; swan-neck spout; leaf-
capped, double "C"-scroll insulated handle.

MEASUREMENTS: H. 22.8 cm (8^{15}/$_{16}$ in); D. base 8.2 cm
(3^1/$_4$ in); W. 24.2 cm (9^1/$_2$ in); WT. 672.1 gm (21.61 oz)

LOAN: *The Holden Family Collection*
Baton Rouge, Louisiana

This coffee pot has a guilloche border, which
also appears on several cups made by Adolphe
Himmel when he was associated with the firm of
A. B. Griswold after the Civil War (see cat. nos.
56 and 59).

15. Coffee and Tea Service   ca. 1850

Pair of Goblets   ca. 1850

MARK (on bottom of bowls): "HYDE & GOODRICH" in rectangle.

DESCRIPTION: Deep bell-shaped bowls; scalloped lips with engraved double arches below; repoussé and chased picturesque landscape around each body with Rococo-revival cartouche; chased, scalloped band on bowls at juncture with shafts; scrolling foliage and flowers around stepped bases; applied, molded feet with beading. "Emile LaSere" engraved in Gothic style in cartouche.

MEASUREMENTS: LEFT: H. 18.5 cm (7$^5/_{16}$ in); D. lip 10.5 cm (4$^1/_8$); D. base 9.1 cm (3$^9/_{16}$ in); WT. 273.2 gm (8.78 oz) RIGHT: H. 18.4 cm (7$^1/_4$ in); D. lip 10.7 cm (4$^3/_{16}$ in); D. base 9.1 cm (3$^9/_{16}$ in); WT. 290.6 gm (9.34 oz)

LOAN: *Private Collection*

Pitcher   ca. 1850

MARKS (on bottom of body): "HYDE & GOODRICH" in rectangle, and; "103" incised.

DESCRIPTION: Rococo-revival bulbous body; scalloped molded lip; flat chased and engraved double arch with bell flowers below lip on body; repoussé and chased scrolled flowers and foliage framing picturesque landscape on either side of body; cartouche under spout; interlocking scrolls surrounding handle juncture with body; leaf-capped, scroll handle terminating in griffin head; applied molded band at base; four pierced foliate scroll and shell feet. "Emile LaSere" engraved in Gothic letters in reserve.

MEASUREMENTS: H. 30.8 cm (12$^1/_{16}$ in); D. base 13.1 cm (5$^1/_8$ in); W. 22.9 cm (9 in); WT. 1010.8 gm (32.50 oz)

LOAN: *Private Collection*

Coffee Pot   ca. 1850

MARKS (on bottom): "HYDE & GOODRICH" in rectangle, and; "101" incised.

DESCRIPTION: Pear-shaped body with lobed neck and lid; flat-chased foliate and floral band encircling lid and top of neck; frame of Rococo-revival scrolls, waves, and flowers forming small reserve and repoussé and chased picturesque vignette; cast melon finial; raised on four pierced scroll and shell ornamental feet; leaf-capped, flat-chased, swan-neck spout; insulated, naturalistic handle with spurs. "Emile LaSere" engraved in Gothic letters in reserve.

MEASUREMENTS: H. 27.2 cm (10$^{11}/_{16}$ in); D. base 10.8 cm (4$^1/_4$ in); W. 27.9 cm (11 in); WT. 1231.7 gm (39.60 oz)

LOAN: *Private Collection*

Tray   ca. 1850

MARKS: None.

DESCRIPTION: Silver-plate-on-copper, rectangular tea tray; Rococo-revival style engraved flat surface forming reserve; cast foliate border on raised rim; scrolled, foliate and shell handles at either end; four molded feet. "Presented/to/Honble Emile LaSere,/member of Congress from Louisiana,/as a testimony of respect and esteem/from grateful friends./Lapeyre Harispe & Co., Jose Prats, Puig y Puig, J. W. Cabellero, R. W. Castillo, Domingo Fatjo./New Orleans, October 14, 1850." engraved in reserve.

MEASUREMENTS: H. 5.7 cm (2$^1/_4$ in); L. 81.9 cm (32 $^1/_4$ in); W. 53.4 cm (21 in)

LOAN: *Private Collection*

As John Slidell's right-hand man during Louisiana's antebellum history, Emile LaSere was a leading Jacksonian Democrat and succeeded Slidell as United States congressman from Louisiana between 1846 and 1851. LaSere was welcomed by the local press upon his return to New Orleans from Washington, D.C., in 1850. About that time he was presented with the large coffee and tea service (only four pieces of which are illustrated) as a gift from a group of New Orleans businessmen in appreciation for his services in securing the repayment of their claims following the Mexican War.

16. Spectacles   ca. 1849

MARKS (on right bow at hinge): "HYDE & GOODRICH"
incised; (on left bow at hinge); "NEW ORLEANS"
incised.

DESCRIPTION: Octagonal, gold frames, enclosing glass,
joined by wide nosepiece; hinged extending temples.

MEASUREMENTS: L. extended 13.6 cm (5³/₈ in); W. 10.6
cm (4³/₈ in); WT. 15.6 gm (.50 oz)

PROVENANCE: These spectacles were bought in 1849 by
James Woodburn, great-great-grandfather of the donors.

Anglo-American Art Museum 76.9.1
Louisiana State University
Baton Rouge, Louisiana
Gift of Miss Ruth Ker Batchelor and Mrs. Clara Bell Douglas

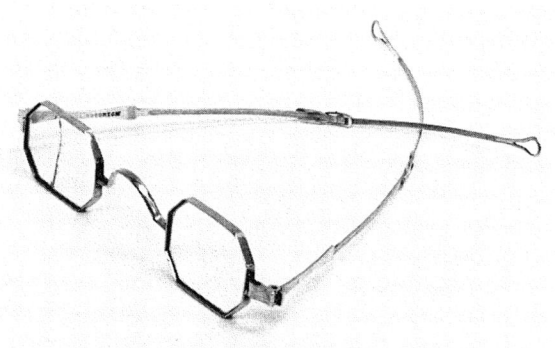

17. Waiter   ca. 1861

MARKS (on bottom): "HYDE & GOODRICH" incised
above; "COIN" incised.

DESCRIPTION: Flat, oval base having molded rim with
applied guilloche border; matte-finished surface engraved with shells and foliage stemming from large oval
scroll reserve; smaller "C"-scroll cartouches on either
end framing picturesque vignettes; raised on four scroll
feet. "Sister Lizzie/from Ben/Dec. 25th, 1864" script
engraving in cartouche.

MEASUREMENTS: H. 2.3 cm (¹⁵/₁₆ in); L. 23.2 cm (10¹/₈
in); W. 18.0 cm (7¹/₁₆ in); WT. 320.0 gm (10.29 oz)

LOAN: *Private Collection*

18.   Serving Tongs   ca. 1850

MARKS (inside, lower shank of fork element):   "X" incised, to right of; "HYDE & GOODRICH" in rectangle.

DESCRIPTION: Double-faced "olive" pattern variant handle terminating in fork and spoon grips. "C.S.P." engraved script monogram on outer juncture of tong shafts.

MEASUREMENTS: H. 24.8 cm (9³/₄ in); W. 10.2 cm (4 in); WT. 174.7 gm (5.61 oz)

Anglo-American Art Museum   79.16.3
Louisiana State University
Baton Rouge, Louisiana
Gift of Mr. and Mrs. Bert S. Turner

The incised "X" on the tongs indicates that they were manufactured in the northeastern United States, probably in New York. A similar pair (see illustration) owned by writer Washington Irving of Tarrytown, New York, was made by William Gale & Son in New York City. After being shipped to the South by local retailers such as Hyde & Goodrich, their general function as a serving piece may have become more specialized. Interviews conducted in 1970 with elderly Natchez, Mississippi, citizens have revealed that tongs of this type were used specifically to serve fried chicken in the nineteenth and early twentieth centuries. Unfortunately, no such tradition has yet been documented in New Orleans.

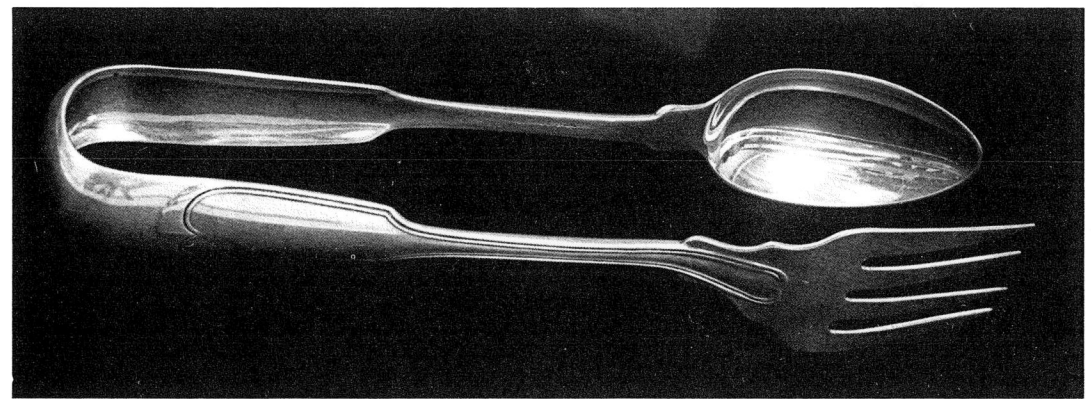

Washington Irving's serving tongs. (Courtesy Sleepy Hollow Restorations, Tarrytown, New York)

19. Crumber   ca. 1855

MARK (on back of handle): "HYDE & GOODRICH" in rectangle.

DESCRIPTION: "Olive" pattern variant handle; crumb plate engraved with scrolling foliage and flowers; scalloped, upturned edges on back and end. "LFL" engraved in script on upper face of handle. Split on upper back of crumb plate near handle and splits around juncture of handle and crumb plate repaired by Christopher A. Hentz.

MEASUREMENTS: L. 33.2 cm (13¹/₈ in); W. 5.4 cm (2¹/₈ in); WT. 159.6 gm (5.13 oz)

Anglo-American Art Museum 79.16.6
Louisiana State University
Baton Rouge, Louisiana
Gift of Mrs. Katherine H. Long

A crumber was considered a necessary utensil for formal dining in America during the Victorian and Edwardian periods. It was used to sweep away food crumbs from the table between each course of the meal. This practice continues in some households and many restaurants today, particularly when diners enjoy the crusty, crumbly French bread of New Orleans.

20. Fish Knife ca. 1850

MARKS (on back of handle): ''X'' incised to right of; ''HYDE & GOODRICH'' in rectangle.

DESCRIPTION: ''Fiddle thread'' handle, straight shoulders; modified scimitar-shaped blade; engraved zigzag border against striated ground and punchwork margin; engraved stylized fish and seaweed on blade; pierced drains. ''Randolph'' engraved in script on upper face of handle.

MEASUREMENTS: L. 29.2 cm (11½ in); W. 7.0 cm (2 ¾ in); WT. 147.2 gm (4.73 oz)

Anglo-American Art Museum   79.16.4
Louisiana State University
Baton Rouge, Louisiana
Gift of the Friends of the Museum

The increasing popularity of specialized serving pieces during the course of the nineteenth century encouraged silver manufacturers to mass-produce established English types. Consequently, the fish knife or slice gained popularity and followed the design of the late eighteenth-century English fish trowel. The skills of the newer age allowed the use of thin silver that could be elaborately pierced and engraved. Most often the center of the blade contained a stylized fish as a symbol of the utensil's function. Both examples were manufactured in the northeastern United States to resemble French silver, which clearly fit the demands of the New Orleans market.

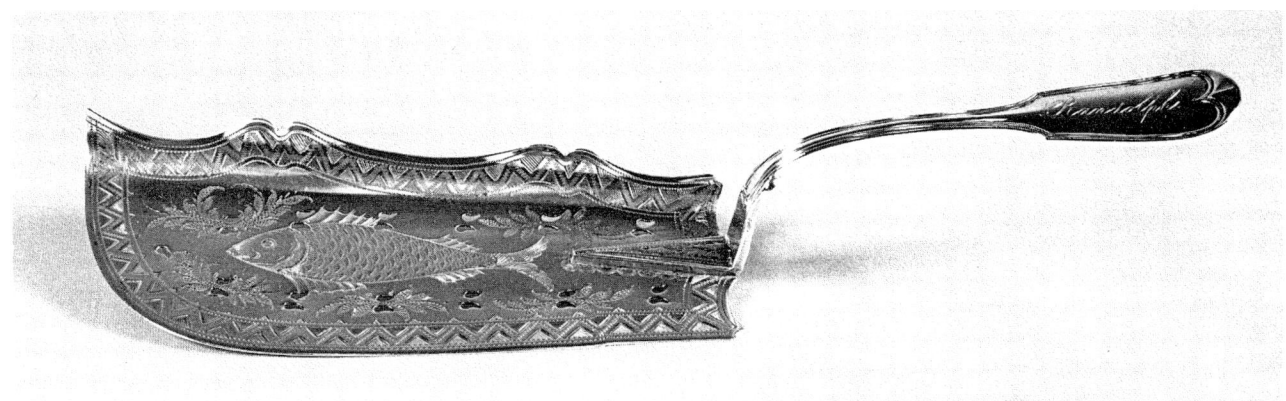

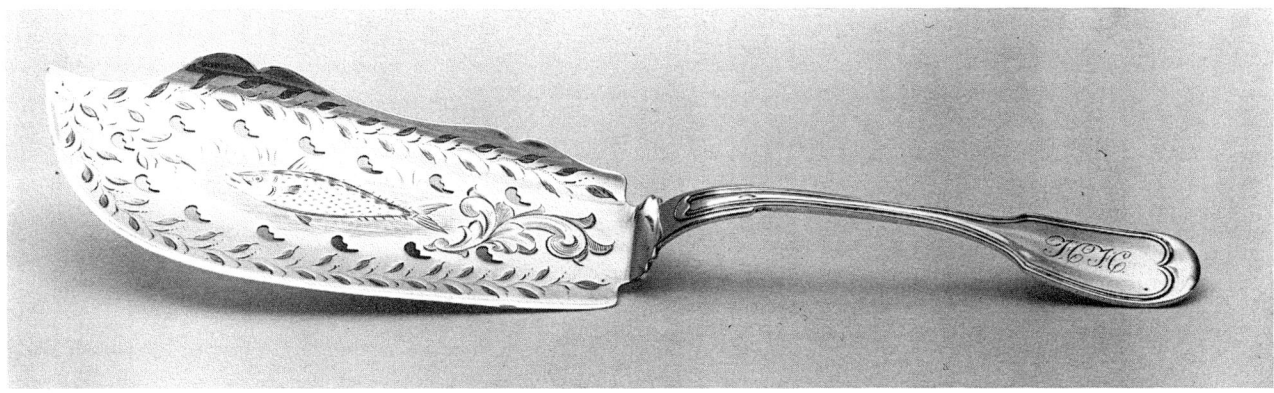

21. Fish Knife ca. 1850

MARKS (on back of handle): ''HYDE & GOODRICH'' incised, to right of; pseudo-hallmarks ''H'', star, and anchor, each in separate punch; (on upper face of handle near blade): star in lozenge.

DESCRIPTION: ''Fiddle thread'' handle with straight shoulders; stylized fish engraved on scimitar-shaped blade surrounded by paisley-shaped pierced drains and engraved foliate border. ''HH'' engraved in script on upper face of handle.

MEASUREMENTS: L. 31.4 cm (12⅜ in); WT. 133.8 gm (4.30 oz)

LOAN: *The Holden Family Collection*
Baton Rouge, Louisiana

22. Butter Knife   ca. 1850

MARKS (on back of handle): "HYDE & GOODRICH" in rectangle, to right of; incised pellet.

DESCRIPTION: "Fiddle thread" handle with single-faced decorative engraving; Rococo-revival cartouche on upper handle; diamond-and-bead band along shank; cross-hatching on shoulder; four rosettes within circles on blade; thread continues around blade. "M.G.McT." engraved script monogram, on upper face of handle.

MEASUREMENTS: L. 19.1 cm (7½ in); WT. 42.2 gm (1.36 oz)

Anglo-American Art Museum   79.16.5
Louisiana State University
Baton Rouge, Louisiana
Gift of the Friends of the Museum

23. Butter Knife   ca. 1850

MARKS (on back of handle): "HYDE & GOODRICH" incised, to right of; "P" incised, to right of; five-pointed star in oval, above; "H" in oval, above; anchor in oval; (on top of handle between shoulders): five-pointed star in lozenge.

DESCRIPTION: "Fiddle thread" handle, straight shoulders; slightly flared scimitar-shaped blade. "G.A.F." engraved in Old English script on back of handle.

MEASUREMENTS: L. 16.6 cm (6⁹⁄₁₆ in); WT. 36.0 gm (1.16 oz)

The Historic New Orleans Collection   1978.175.36.1
New Orleans, Louisiana

Large butter knives were passed with the butter plate or with the butter cooler (see cat. no. 114) and allowed each diner to serve himself.

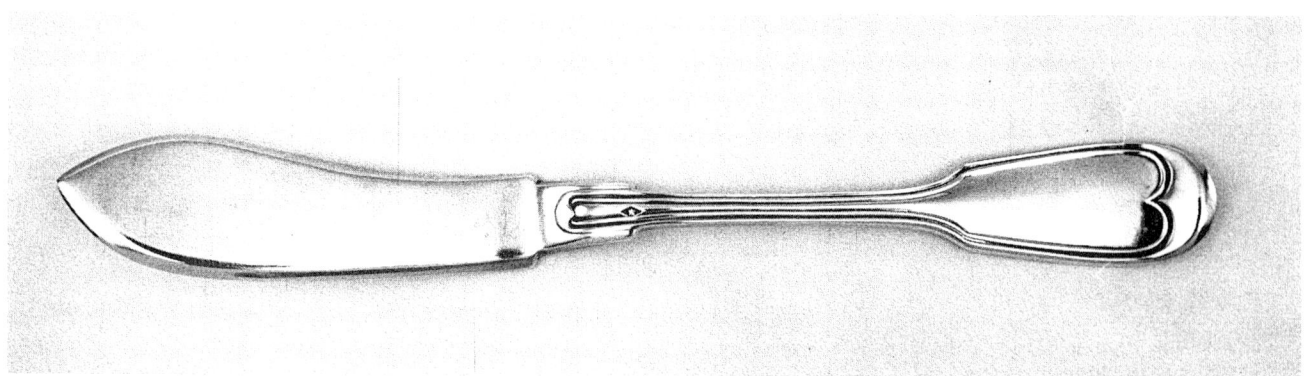

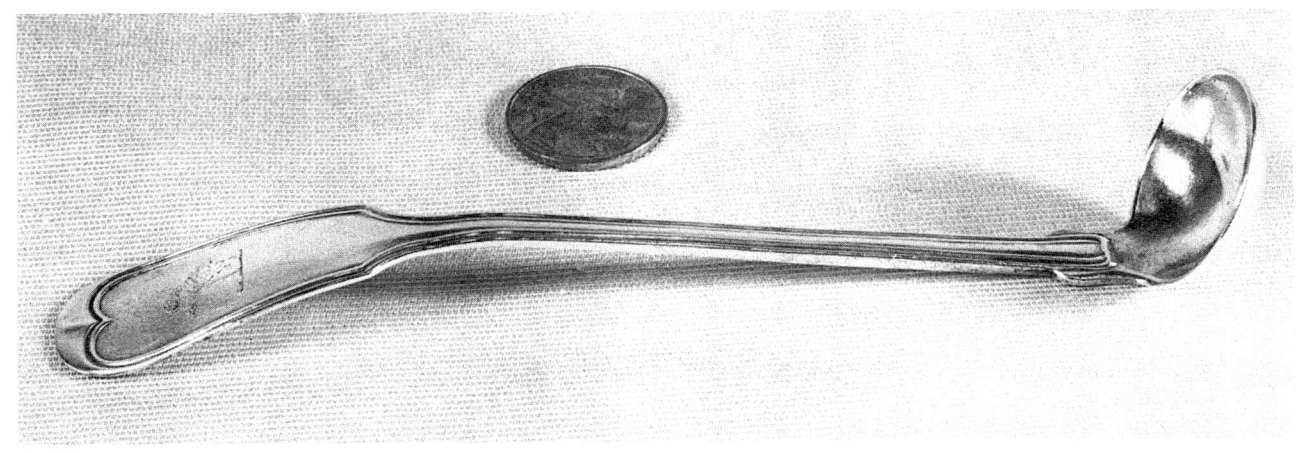

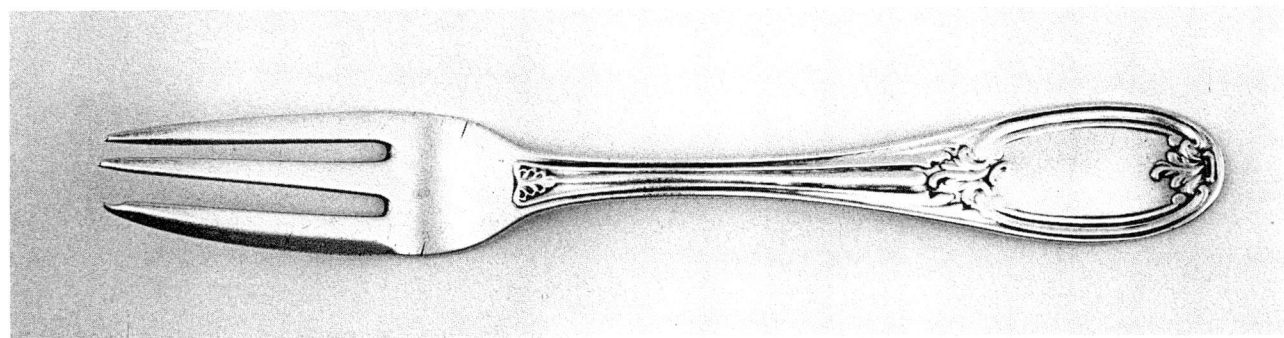

24. Mustard Spoon   ca. 1845

MARKS (on back of handle): "HYDE & GOODRICH" in rectangle, to right of; S-shaped symbol.

DESCRIPTION: Small, "fiddle thread" handle with curved shoulders at juncture with round bowl. Engraved crest on upper face of handle: oak tree to left of lion rampant, facing right.

MEASUREMENTS: L. 13.4 cm (5¼ in); D. bowl 2.4 cm (¹⁵/₁₆ in); WT. 17.3 gm (.56 oz)

Anglo-American Art Museum   79.16.2
Louisiana State University
Baton Rouge, Louisiana
Gift of the Friends of the Museum

Condiments served with meals became increasingly popular during the nineteenth century. Louisiana's well-seasoned cuisine could always be made spicier at the table with the addition of products such as dry or prepared mustard, kept in a mustard pot with an opening in its lid for a spoon. Numerous examples of these small ladle-like utensils survive, especially in the "fiddle" and the "fiddle thread" patterns.

25. Celery Fork   ca. 1847

MARKS (on back of handle): "PATENT 1847." incised, to left of; "O" incised, to left of; "HYDE & GOOD-RICH" incised.

DESCRIPTION: Three-tine fork in "olive" pattern variation; outer tine slightly wider and shaped for cutting blade. "Ashbridge." engraved in script on back of handle.

MEASUREMENTS: L. 15.4 cm (6¹/₁₆ in); WT. 32.5 gm (1.04 oz)

The Historic New Orleans Collection   1978.175.89
New Orleans, Louisiana

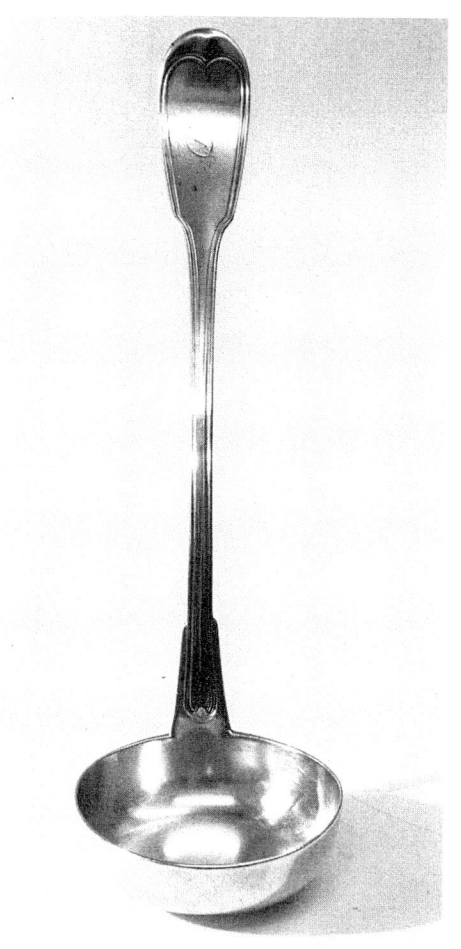
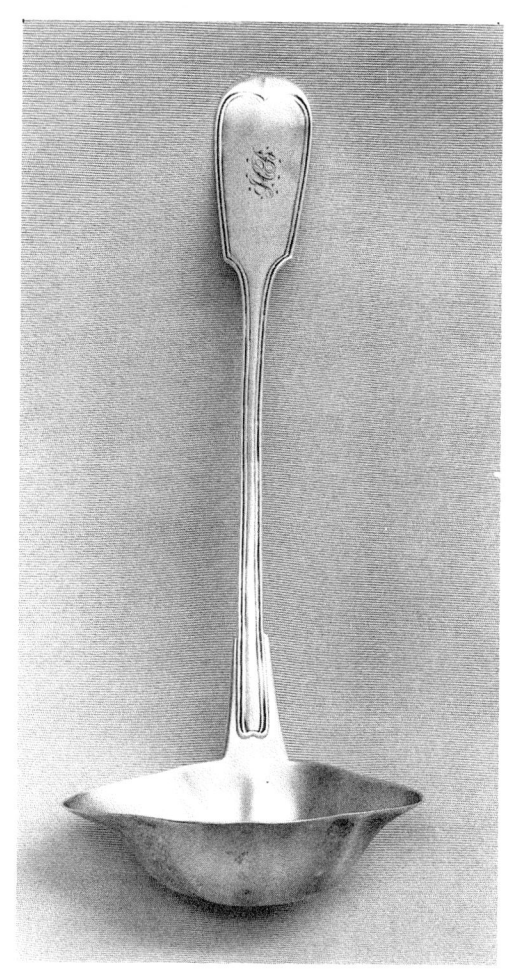

26. Ladle   ca. 1845-1860

> MARKS (on back of handle): "HYDE & GOODRICH" in rectangle, to right of; incised check mark.

> DESCRIPTION: "Fiddle thread" handle, straight shoulders; broad, flat bowl in continental manner. "LC" engraved script cipher monogram on upper face of handle.

> MEASUREMENTS: L. 31.8 cm (12½ in); D. bowl 8.5 cm (3⅜ in); WT. 234.8 gm (7.55 oz)

> PROVENANCE: The initials, "LC", are those of one of the members of the Chopin family who settled in Natchitoches Parish, Louisiana, in the early nineteenth century.

> LOAN: *Private Collection*

27. Punch Ladle   ca. 1855

> MARKS (on back of handle): "HYDE & GOODRICH" in rectangle, to right of; "O" incised, partially rubbed.

> DESCRIPTION: "Fiddle thread" handle, straight shoulders; shaped, oval bowl with two spouts. "PCB" engraved script monogram on upper face of handle.

> MEASUREMENTS: L. 33.6 cm (13¼ in); D. bowl 11.8 cm (4⅝ in); WT. 170.6 gm (5.49 oz)

> LOAN: *Private Collection*

While most of the ladles in the exhibition were designed for serving soup (see cat. no. 26), this ladle, with its double-spouted bowl, was intended for serving punch.

28. Ladle after 1865
Dessert Fork, Dinner Fork, Tablespoon, Dessert Spoon, and Teaspoon ca. 1855-1861

MARKS (on back of handle of forks and spoons): "HYDE & GOODRICH" incised, to right of; unidentified doublestruck incised mark; "PATENT 1855" and curious marks "E" (on dinner fork), crescent (on dessert spoon), and "C" (on others) incised; (on back of handle of ladle): "J. P. PATENT 1855" and "A. B. GRISWOLD" incised.

DESCRIPTION: "Oriental" pattern handles. "S" engraved in Gothic letters on reverse of each.

MEASUREMENTS: LADLE: L. 31.8 cm (12½ in); D. bowl 10.3 cm (4¹/₁₆ in); WT. 206.1 gm (6.63 oz) DESSERT FORK: L. 17.7 cm (6¹⁵/₁₆ in); WT. 51.3 gm (1.65 oz) DINNER FORK: L. 19.7 cm (7³/₄ in); WT. 72.5 gm (2.33 oz) TABLESPOON: L. 21.5 cm (8⁷/₁₆ in); WT. 77.0 gm (2.48 oz) DESSERT SPOON: L. 17.7 cm (6¹⁵/₁₆ in); WT. 56.2 gm (1.81 oz) TEASPOON: L. 15.2 cm (5¹⁵/₁₆ in); WT. 38.9 gm (1.25 oz)

The Historic New Orleans Collection 1976.103.1, 13, 25, 37,
New Orleans, Louisiana 49, 61

It was the practice among merchants in New Orleans to retail flatware produced and patented on the east coast. This silver indicates just that, for the maker's marks appear to be those of either Newell Harding & Co., of Boston, or H. Hebbard & Co., of New York. The other curious marks and letters stamped over an indistinguishable mark may represent unrecoded date letters or weights. The pattern, identified as "Oriental," was patented by John Polhemus of New York. He also manufactured silver for Tiffany & Co. in New York and for E. A. Tyler in New Orleans (cat. no. 103). Characteristic of the era, the set mixes pieces retailed by both Hyde & Goodrich and its successor firm, A. B. Griswold & Co. That the owners of the set added pieces years after the original purchases attests to the continued popularity of this exotic pattern.

TIFFANY, YOUNG AND ELLIS

The New York establishment of Tiffany, Young & Ellis was a partnership from 1841 to 1853, of Charles Tiffany, John B. Young, and J. L. Ellis. During the period from 1847 to 1851, Tiffany, Young & Ellis retailed silver from a number of New York silversmiths including John C. Moore and Wood & Hughes. In 1853, the firm became Tiffany & Co.

The silver designs of John C. Moore and Tiffany & Co. were drawn upon by New Orleans silversmiths during the 1850s. Those manufacturing silver for Hyde & Goodrich were either "matching" or "improving" upon the New York examples.

29. Coffee and Tea Service   ca. 1850

MARK (on bottom of bowl of each piece): "TIFFANY, YOUNG & ELLIS/J.C.M." incised.

DESCRIPTION: Late Federal or Georgian shapes decorated with Rococo-revival style foliage; bird finials where appropriate. "Lyle" engraved in Gothic lettering on side of body of each piece. The handle for the sugar basket, the heat rings of the coffee pot, and a silver pin in the handle of the kettle-on-stand are carefully made reconstructions by Herbert Gebelein.

MEASUREMENTS: KETTLE-ON-STAND: H. 33.0 cm (13 in); WT. 1673.1 gm (53.79 oz) COFFEE POT: H. 23.5 cm (9¼ in); D. base: 9.2 cm (3⅝ in); WT. 851.7 gm (27.38 oz) TEA POT: H. 15.2 cm (6 in); D. base 10.8 cm (4¼ in); WT. 820.5 gm (26.38 oz) WASTE BOWL: H. 10.2 cm (4¼ in); D. base 8.5 cm (3⅜ in); WT. 347.7 gm (11.18 oz) SUGAR BOWL: 13.3 cm (5¼ in); D. base 8.9 cm (3½ in); WT. 518.2 gm (16.66 oz) CREAMER: H. 17.1 cm (6¾ in); D. base 7.0 cm (2¾ in); WT. 329.0 gm (10.58 oz) SUGAR BASKET: H. 12.4 cm (4⅞ in); D. base 6.3 cm (2½ in); WT. 213.6 gm (6.87 oz)

PROVENANCE: Made for Dr. and Mrs. William Jones Lyle of Smithfield Plantation in West Baton Rouge Parish, Louisiana. Dr. Lyle also owned property in New Orleans and West Feliciana Parish. He was buried on April 18, 1863, in Grace Episcopal Church Cemetery, St. Francisville, Louisiana.

Anglo-American Art Museum   76.23.1-7
Louisiana State University
Baton Rouge, Louisiana
Gift of Major General Junius Wallace Jones

Similar to the practice with flatware, local firms also retailed silver hollowware in popular designs that had originated in the eastern United States. The design of this particular set combines the shapes and silhouettes in late Classical pieces with the chased decorations in Rococo-revival. Around 1850, this already large service was supplemented with a matching hot water pitcher and a hot milk pitcher. Both pieces are marked on the bottom "HYDE & GOODRICH." Another coffee and tea service, made for David Cohen Labatt of New Orleans, shows the same design. However, it was made in Boston by Vincent Laforme & Bro. and retailed through Hyde & Goodrich in New Orleans. Apparently, both New York and Boston manufacturers supplied New Orleans's retailers with silver services and parts of services that were then marked and sold by the local company.

Hot water and hot milk pitchers. (Courtesy Mrs. Virgil A. Robinson, Jr.)

Labatt sugar bowl and creamer. (Courtesy *Southern Silver* catalogue, 1968, Museum of Fine Arts, Houston, Texas)

30. Coffee and Tea Service   ca. 1850

MARKS (on bottom of each piece): "T.Y.& E." in rectangle; (additional mark on creamer): "W & H" in oval.

DESCRIPTION: Inverted pear-shaped bodies supported on stepped circular bases; three applied shell-and-acanthus-leaf borders at lip, shoulder, and as foot of each piece; water-leaf border at lip of each piece (except creamer); domed lids with urn-shaped finials (except creamer); one side engraved with views of St. Charles Hotel, other side with floral and foliate wreath forming reserve; "S"-scroll silver handles with spur thumbpieces; swan-neck spouts. "St. Charles Hotel Plate/won by/Flying Dutchman/2 Mile Heats-Metaire Course/Time/3.45. 3.42/Nov. 23 1850" engraved within reserves.

MEASUREMENTS: COFFEE POT: H. 33.0 cm (13 in); D. base 12.1 cm (4³/₄ in); W. 26.7 cm (10¹/₂ in); WT. 1041.1 gm (33.47 oz) TEA POT: H. 27.9 cm (11 in); D. base 11.4 cm (4¹/₂ in); W. 26.7 cm (10¹/₂ in); WT. 891.0 gm (28.65 oz) SUGAR BOWL: H. 24.8 cm (9³/₄ in); D. base 10.2 cm (4 in); W. 19.1 cm (7¹/₂ in); WT. 794.1 gm (25.53 oz) CREAMER: H. 20.9 cm (8¹/₄ in); D. base 8.5 cm (3³/₈ in); W. 15.9 cm (6¹/₄ in); WT. 382.0 gm (12.28 oz)

LOAN: *Private Collection*

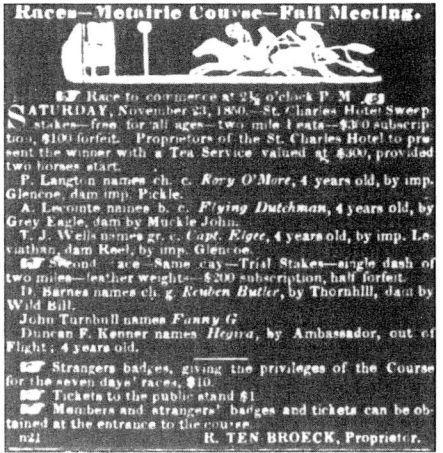

Newspaper article announcing St. Charles Sweepstakes. *Daily Picayune*, 23 November 1850.

Horse racing has always been a popular sport in New Orleans. From 1838 the elliptical track at the Metairie Race Course offered a regular racing schedule. The St. Charles Hotel Sweepstakes, run on November 23rd, was the first race of the 1850 season at the Metairie Race Course. It was sponsored by the proprietors of that famous hotel, which dominated the New Orleans skyline from the time it opened in 1836. Each piece of the service is engraved with a view of the St. Charles Hotel, the first of three to bear the name and to occupy the site. This handsome Neo-classical structure was destroyed by fire on January 18, 1851. The vignettes on the presentation service may be the last images of the original edifice executed while it was standing; they were engraved only three months before its demise.

KÜCHLER & HIMMEL

The impressed "K & H" mark appearing on some pieces of Hyde & Goodrich silver is the initials of the New Orleans partnership Küchler & Himmel, between two Germans, Christopf Christian Küchler and Adolphe Himmel.

However productive, the partnership was extremely short-lived, active only during 1852 and 1853. The partnership did not make silver exclusively for Hyde & Goodrich. At least one example is known of a Küchler & Himmel piece not marked by a retailer.

31. Beaker ca. 1852-1853

MARK (on bottom): "K & H" in rectangle.

DESCRIPTION: Round body; applied molded lip and foot; signs of engine turning on base. "AW & NAG" engraved in script on side of body.

MEASUREMENTS: H. 8.8 cm (3⁷/₁₆ in) D. lip 7.4 cm (2⁷/₈ in); D. base 6.3 cm (2¹/₂ in); WT. 102.3 gm (3.29 oz)

Anglo-American Art Museum 78.17
Louisiana State University
Baton Rouge, Louisiana
Gift of the Friends of the Museum

The beaker is one of the few examples of a Küchler & Himmel piece without Hyde & Goodrich marks.

32. Coffee Pot ca. 1852-1853

MARKS (on bottom): "HYDE & GOODRICH" in arc, above; "MANUFACTURERS" in rectangle, above; "NEW ORLEANS" in complementary arc. "WARRANTED/PURE COIN" in scalloped rectangle with pointed ends formed by anthemia, at right angle with; "K & H" in rectangle.

DESCRIPTION: Pear-shaped body with repoussé and chased "C"-scrolls, diapering, shells, and foliage; low, fluted, domed lid with cast melon finial; applied splayed foot with inverted papyrus-and-leaf border; curved, octagonal spout; leaf-capped, double "C"-scroll, insulated handle.

MEASUREMENTS: H. 24.1 cm (9½ in); D. base 10.1 cm (4¼ in); W. 25.3 cm (10 in); WT. 801.3 gm (25.76 oz)

LOAN: *Private Collection*

This coffee pot is similar in design to the coffee and tea service made by Adolphe Himmel for Hyde & Goodrich (cat. no. 44). The same applied border at the base of the coffee pot is also apparent on the Küchler & Himmel goblet (cat. no. 34).

33. Hot Milk Pitcher   ca. 1852-1853

MARKS (on bottom): "HYDE & GOODRICH" in rectangle, below; "K & H" in oval.

DESCRIPTION: Octagonal body; lip and base with applied molding; conforming domed, hinged lid with finial and thumbpiece; repoussé and chased foliage and flowers on body; foliage, flowers, and scrolls on covered spout and lid; insulated scroll handle with leaf-shaped thumbpiece.

MEASUREMENTS: H. 21.3 cm (8³/₈ in); W. 21.6 cm (8¹/₂ in); WT. 832.2 gm (26.76 oz)

Anglo-American Art Museum   79.16.15
Louisiana State University
Baton Rouge, Louisiana
Gift of Coca-Cola Bottling Works of Baton Rouge

Café au lait is as popular a beverage in southern Louisiana as it is in France. To serve it properly, one must simultaneously pour black coffee from one pot and hot milk from another pot into a serving cup. Hot milk pitchers are distinguished from creamers by ivory or bone insulators needed to keep the handle cool. The lid and the partially-covered spout retained the heat of the milk inside and kept insects from the contents. Hot milk pitchers were not normally part of a service, but were accessories sometimes added to an existing set.

32

34. Goblet   ca. 1852-1853

MARKS (on bottom of bowl): "HYDE & GOODRICH"
in arc, above; "K & H" in oval, above; "NEW
ORLEANS" in complementary arc.

DESCRIPTION: Bulbous bowl on high-stepped base; applied beaded border below lip; repoussé cabbage
roses and leaves around body with Rococo-revival
cartouche on one side; repoussé flowers and leaves on
top of base; applied inverted papyrus-and-leaf border as
vertical foot.

MEASUREMENTS: H. 14.0 cm (5½ in); D. lip 8.9 cm
(3½ in); D. base 7.25 cm (2 ⅞ in); WT. 155.9 gm
(5.01 oz)

Anglo-American Art Museum   71.13.1
Louisiana State University
Baton Rouge, Louisiana
Gift of Mr. and Mrs. William T. Baynard

35. Cup   ca. 1852-1853

MARKS (on bottom): "HYDE & GOODRICH" in arc,
above; "K & H" in oval.

DESCRIPTION: Small round body; straight sides tapered
from lip with applied molding; beading below curved
base with flat, slightly domed bottom; gilt wash inside
bowl; flat, scroll handle with thumbpiece. "Sidney/to
Alice Elizabeth" engraved on body.

MEASUREMENTS: H. 4.9 cm (1¹⁵⁄₁₆ in); D. lip 5.9 cm
2⁵⁄₁₆ in); D. base 4.4 cm (1¹¹⁄₁₆ in); W. 8.0 cm (3¼
in); WT. 46.6 gm (1.50 oz)

The Historic New Orleans Collection   1978.175.13
New Orleans, Louisiana

36. Pitcher   ca. 1852-1853

MARKS (on base of body): "HYDE & GOODRICH" in arc,
above; "MANUFACTURERS" in rectangle, above;
"NEW ORLEANS. LA" in complementary arc;
"K & H" in oval; "WARRANTED/PURE COIN"
in scalloped rectangle with pointed ends formed by
anthemia.

DESCRIPTION: Bulbous, pear-shaped body; repoussé and
chased scrolling foliage with flowers just under lip and
on body forming cartouche on either side; molded flared
foot; naturalistic twig-like handle.

MEASUREMENTS: H. 22.8 cm (9 in); D. base 12.8 cm
(5 in); W. 23.8 cm (9³/₈ in); WT. 422.9 gm (13.60 oz)

The Historic New Orleans Collection   1978.175.11
New Orleans, Louisiana

This Küchler & Himmel piece is the earliest
of four similar pitchers retailed by Hyde & Goodrich. Slight variations distinguish the later pitchers
by C. C. Küchler and by A. Himmel, after the

former partners were working separately (cat. nos.
40, 53); while the development of the Rococo-revival style culminated in the extraordinary Badgett
family pitcher (cat. no. 54), by Himmel alone.

American craftsmen working in the Rococo-
revival style invented newer forms within the flam-
boyant mode than those of their European contemporaries. American interpretation was strongly
influenced in ornamentation and in form by naturalistic elements such as grapevines, grape clusters,
oak leaves, acorns, roses, fruits, and vegetables.
The pear-shaped, low-slung, almost bulbous
shapes of the vessels' bodies were embellished with
the finest repoussé and chased work of the period.
Additional touches were added by cast, naturalistic
finials and handles.

The Rococo-revival style continued to be im-
mensely popular in New Orleans well into the
1860s, when the Badgett pitcher (cat. no. 54) and
the Rondeau family tureen (cat. no. 55) were made.

CHRISTOPF CHRISTIAN KÜCHLER

The impressed "K" between scrolled brackets is the touchmark of Christopf Christian Küchler. Very little is known of Küchler. He first appears in the New Orleans city directories for 1852, and then in the short-lived partnership with Adolphe Himmel. He later formed a partnership with Bernard Terfloth in 1858. After the Civil War, he worked with August Jansen.

His correct first name appears in the death certificate of Küchler's daughter on information given, sworn to, and subscribed by Küchler. His wife, Wilhelmine Schmidt Küchler, died December 28, 1867, aged thirty-nine years, and was buried in Greenwood Cemetery, New Orleans.

It is unlikely that Küchler at any time during his New Orleans career manufactured silver exclusively for Hyde & Goodrich. The impressed "C. Küchler" mark appears on a number of objects from a diminutive hollow handle cake trowel to a remarkably ornate fireman's trumpet.

37. Pitcher ca. 1853-1858

MARKS (on base of body): "HYDE & GOODRICH" in arc, above; "MANUFACTURERS" in rectangle, above; "NEW ORLEANS. LA" in complementary arc; "K" between scrolled brackets in conforming cartouche; "WARRANTED/PURE COIN" in scalloped rectangle with pointed ends formed by anthemia.

DESCRIPTION: Baluster-shaped body; molded lip with fleur-de-lis banding; repoussé and chased acanthus border under lip and around base; repoussé and chased foliate wreath on four sides stemming from "C"-scrolls and foliage in shape of fleur-de-lis; picturesque landscape vignette in reserve under spout; applied vertical foot with stylized foliate and hatchet band. "MSB" engraved in script cipher monogram inside reserve.

MEASUREMENTS: H. 26.0 cm (10¼ in); D. base 12.4 cm (4⅞ in); W. 24.1 cm (9½ in); WT. 845.1 gm (27.17 oz)

LOAN: *Mrs. Jack C. Brier*
Sacramento, California

38. Cup   ca. 1855

MARKS (on bottom): "HYDE & GOODRICH" in arc, above; "MANUFACTURERS" in rectangle, above; "K" between scrolled brackets in conforming cartouche, above; "NEW ORLEANS. LA" in complementary arc.

DESCRIPTION: Round body; straight sides curved at base; lip with applied molding and beading; band of palmette, ball-and-string motif against striated ground on applied flared foot; flat-chased grapevine arbor forming cartouche on body opposite scroll handle with thumbpiece. "AJ/to/AJP" engraved in cartouche.

MEASUREMENTS: H. 8.3 cm (3¹/₄ in); D. lip and base 5.3 cm (2¹/₁₆ in); W. 8.6 cm (3³/₈ in); WT. 85.7 gm (2.76 oz)

The Historic New Orleans Collection   1978.175.18
New Orleans, Louisiana

39. Cup   ca. 1855

MARKS (on bottom): "HYDE & GOODRICH" in arc, above; "MANUFACTURERS" in rectangle, above; "NEW ORLEANS. LA" in complementary arc, above; "K" between scrolled brackets in conforming cartouche.

DESCRIPTION: Round body decorated with four flat-chased arbors with vines, two arbors with hanging baskets of flowers; lip with applied molding and beading; flared foot with applied molding and beading; leaf-capped double "C"-scroll handle. "Edw. & E. Trice./from/E. H. Dix" engraved in script in arbor opposite handle.

MEASUREMENTS: H. 12.5 cm (4⁷/₈ in); D. lip 9.0 cm (3¹/₂ in); D. base 7.1 cm (2³/₄ in); WT. 258.6 gm (8.31 oz)

The Historic New Orleans Collection   1978.175.21
New Orleans, Louisiana

40. Pitcher   ca. 1853-1855

MARKS (on base of body): "HYDE & GOODRICH" in arc, above; "MANUFACTURERS" in rectangle, above; "NEW ORLEANS, LA" in complementary arc, above; "WARRANTED/PURE COIN" in scalloped rectangle with pointed ends formed by anthemia; "K" between scrolled brackets in conforming cartouche, upside down above Hyde and Goodrich mark.

DESCRIPTION: Bulbous pear-shaped body; repoussé and chased scrolling foliage with flowers forming two car-

touches of "C"-scrolls, waves, and leaves; rim and foot with applied molding; chased flowers and foliage under lip and on spout; naturalistic twig-like handle.

MEASUREMENTS: H. 21.3 cm (8³/₈ in); D. base 12.6 cm (4¹⁵/₁₆ in); W. 23.5 cm (9¹/₄ in); WT. 854.3 gm (27.47 oz)

LOAN: *Private Collection*

TERFLOTH & KÜCHLER

The partnership of Terfloth & Küchler was comprised of Bernard Terfloth and Christopf Christian Küchler. It was active from 1858 to 1866.

Terfloth was born in Greven R.R., Münster, Prussia, about 1829. He first appeared in New Orleans in 1858. Following the dissolution of the partnership, Terfloth continued to work in New Orleans until 1870.

Terfloth & Küchler seem to have specialized in fine presentation pieces. They do not appear to have been a very productive firm; however, they frequently marked only individual parts in the elaborate sets, and not each object.

View of top and detail of side of tea tray presented to Colonel James B. Walton by the Washington Artillery, showing field cannon motifs used as feet, and with mortar and cannon ball decoration around lip. (Courtesy Private Collection, photograph by Jean Jeffers)

41. Pair of Goblets   ca. 1859

MARKS: none.

DESCRIPTION: Globular bowls on high baluster-shaped stems and splayed domed bases; molded lips with beading; repoussé water-leaf band around base of each bowl; repoussé and chased emblematic military vignette on one side of each body, presentation shield with flags on opposite side; larger, cast beads, as cannon balls, applied to upper part of molded foot. "Presented/to/Captn James B. Walton/by the/Officers and Members/of the/Washington Artillery/New Orleans. Nov./30th 1859." engraved in script on each cup. Both goblets were straightened and dents knocked out by Christopher A. Hentz.

MEASUREMENTS: LEFT: H. 23.0 cm (9^1/$_{16}$ in); D. lip 9.9 cm (3^7/$_8$ in); D. base 8.9 cm (3^1/$_2$ in); WT. 354.1 gm (11.38 oz) RIGHT: H. 23.2 cm (9^1/$_8$ in); D. lip 9.7 cm (3^{13}/$_{16}$ in); D. base 8.9 cm (3^1/$_2$ in); WT. 365.5 gm (11.75 oz)

PROVENANCE: The Washington Artillery of New Orleans is the oldest military organization in the state of Louisiana. It was organized in 1839 through the influence of Persifor F. Smith, later general and hero of Contreras during the Mexican War. On February 22, 1840, it was reorganized as the Right Flank Company of the Washington Regiment, being the only military organization in the American quarter of the city. In 1844, James B. Walton was a lieutenant colonel of this regiment and in 1846, when it entered the service of the United States, Lieutenant Colonel Walton was in command of the regiment. After serving under General Zachary Taylor in the Rio Grande Campaign, and returning to New Orleans, Colonel Walton was elected Captain of the Artillery Battalion. At the beginning of the Civil War, the command was increased to four companies or batteries and moved immediately to the seat of the war in Virginia. J. B. Walton was made Chief of Artillery, Army of the Potomac, in November, 1861; Chief of Artillery, Longstreet's Corps; appointed by Secretary of War, Inspector-General of Field Artillery; recommended twice by Generals Beauregard and Longstreet for promotion to Brigadier General of Artillery; and resigned, July, 1864. J. B. Walton returned to command the Washington Artillery again in the 1870s.

LOAN: *Private Collection*

Colonel James B. Walton. Detail of 1861 wash drawing. (Courtesy Louisiana Historical Association, Confederate Memorial Hall, New Orleans)

The description of the silver service which appeared on the front page of the *New Orleans Bee* for Friday, December 2, 1859, documents its original size and identifies Terfloth and Küchler as the silversmiths—a fact confirmed by the marks on the salver.

The service was one of the richest, most appropriate and artistically gotten up of any thing we ever saw of the kind. The salver was supported on four miniature cannons, of gold and silver, the minutest appointments of the guns being faithfully wrought. The rim was ornamented with a row of cannon balls and bombs, of graduated size, relieved at intervals with gold mortars and piles of balls. The surface was beautifully engraved with the inscription, the State coat of arms and insignia of the company, supported on one side by the eagle of America and on the other by the pelican of Louisiana. The goblets were of silver, lined with gold, and like the pitcher, ornamented with the inscription, and appropriate embellishments in relief and engraved. The service is a splendid piece of skillful workmenship, and reflects the highest credit upon the artists, Messrs. Terfloth and Kuchler of this city.

The engraved vignette in the center of the tray conforms to the design on the goblets. The gilding is still in good condition on the goblets, but has worn off the salver. The pitcher has not been located.

42. Covered Pitcher   ca. 1850

MARKS (on bottom): "TERFLOTH & KUECHLER"
    incised in arc, above; "NEW ORLEANS" in com-
    plementary arc.

DESCRIPTION: Pear-shaped body; covered spout with
    hinged tip; hinged, flat-domed lid; elaborately orna-
    mented cast finial; applied flared foot with stylized
    foliate and hatchet banding; "C"-scroll handle.

MEASUREMENTS: H. 19.9 cm (7⅞ in); D. base 9.7 cm
    (3¹¹/₁₆ in); W. 18.7 cm (7⁵/₁₆ in); WT. 501.0 gm (16.11 oz)

LOAN: *Elizabeth Pipes Wingfield*
    New Orleans, Louisiana

ADOLPHE HIMMEL

The large incised "H" appearing on Hyde & Goodrich pieces is the mark of Adolphe Himmel. Himmel, according to family tradition, was born in Zweibrücken, Germany. For reasons now obscure, but undoubtedly connected with the political turmoil in 1848, he left Germany and changed his name to Himmel in order to escape detection. He was so thorough in obscuring his true identity that his actual surname has not yet been discovered.

Himmel first appears in the New Orleans directories for 1852, in partnership with Christopf Christian Küchler. This partnership, although active only briefly, produced pieces bearing only the Küchler & Himmel mark, as well as those articles retailed through Hyde & Goodrich. In 1853, the partnership was dissolved. Himmel began manufacturing exclusively for Hyde & Goodrich, but he was not the sole supplier to the firm. Pieces from this period also bear the mark of Küchler. After 1855, Himmel's operation on the corner of Bienville and Derbigny Streets appears to have been the exclusive supplier of locally-made hollowware for Hyde & Goodrich and its successor, Thomas, Griswold & Co., later A.B. Griswold & Co. Himmel continued as chief silversmith for A.B. Griswold & Co. until roughly 1869.

In 1869, Himmel moved his operations from the corner of Bienville and Derbigny Streets to Poydras Street, and worked there until his death in 1877. Himmel's business was taken over by Henry Hausmann, a former business associate of Himmel.

Himmel is known to have traveled to New York. Certain of his designs are evidently based on pieces produced by Tiffany, Young & Ellis and Tiffany & Co. of New York during the 1850s.

Adolphe Himmel and his wife. Undated photographs. (Courtesy Mrs. Frances Grabe)

43. Cup ca. 1853

MARKS (on bottom): "HYDE & GOODRICH" incised in arc, above; "H" incised and on its side, above; "NEW ORLEANS" incised in complementary arc.

DESCRIPTION: Cylindrical body terminating in round base on applied flared foot with arabesque foliate banding; four engraved, double-arch panels, two side panels containing repoussé floral sprays; simple curved handle with thumbpiece. "A/Doctor Moss/Souvenir de Reconnaissance/de/M H B/1853" engraved in script on panel opposite handle.

MEASUREMENTS: H. 8.8 cm (3½ in); D. lip 8.1 cm 3³/₁₆ in); D. base 6.6 cm (2⁵/₈ in); W. 11.4 cm (4½ in); WT. 236.5 gm (7.60 oz)

PROVENANCE: A Dr. B. H. Moss is listed at 158 Canal Street in the 1853 city directory. Dr. B. H. Moss died in New Orleans, 1873, aged 55 years.

Anglo-American Art Museum 79.16.13
Louisiana State University
Baton Rouge, Louisiana
Gift of Mrs. Katherine H. Long

This coffee and tea service follows the same
general design as the coffee pot made by Himmel
(cat. no. 32), varying only in details of decoration.
The applied foot is the same type as the one on the
Badgett pitcher (cat. no. 54). The original creamer
was replaced by T. Hausmann & Sons.

44. Coffee and Tea Service   ca. 1855

MARKS (on bottom of coffee pot, tea pot, and sugar bowl):
"HYDE & GOODRICH" incised in arc, above; "H"
incised, above; "NEW ORLEANS" incised in complementary arc; (on base of creamer): "T. HAUSMANN
& SONS" incised above; "STERLING" incised.

DESCRIPTION: Pear-shaped bodies; chased band of oak
leaves encircling necks of upper lobed sections; conforming domed, hinged lid (unhinged on sugar bowl, none on
creamer) with cast acorn and oak leaf finial;
repoussé and chased acorns and oak leaves ornamenting
bodies and swan-neck spout; applied flared vertical foot
of running curule-and-cross banding; ornate double
"C"-scroll insulated (except sugar bowl) handles.

MEASUREMENTS: COFFEE POT: H. 23.5 cm (9¼ in);
D. base 12.0 cm (4¾ in); W. 26.1 cm (10¼ in);
WT. 897.0 gm (28.84 oz) TEA POT: H. 21.0 cm (8¼

in); D. base 11.1 cm (4³/₈ in); W. 25.8 cm (10¹/₈ in);
WT. 810.2 gm (26.05 oz) SUGAR BOWL: H.
17.1 cm (6¾ in); D. base 10.2 cm (4 in); W. 20.4 cm
(8 in); WT. 590.5 gm (18.99 oz) CREAMER:
H. 14.6 cm (5 ³/₄ in); D. base 8.9 cm (3¹/₂ in); W. 17.2
cm (6³/₄ in); WT. 350.1 gm (11.26 oz)

PROVENANCE: This coffee and tea service is believed to
have been originally owned by Daniel Polk Logan.
Logan was born in Charleston, South Carolina, in 1812.
He moved to New Orleans where he was a cotton brok-
er. In 1843, he married Miss Martha Burton in New
Orleans.

LOAN: *Katharine Logan Forsyth*
New York, New York

45. Goblet   ca. 1855

MARKS (on base of bowl): "HYDE & GOODRICH" incised in arc, above; "H" incised, above, "NEW
ORLEANS" incised in complementary arc.

DESCRIPTION: Globular bowl with beading just below
lip; spool-shaped shaft; circular stepped base with
beaded border above convex molded foot and two
borders of punchwork on lower and upper steps.
"J B Lyman/to/Dr. Wm Harper/Epidemic of 1855"
engraved in script on one side of bowl.

MEASUREMENTS: H. 16.3 cm (6³/₈ in); D. lip 9.0 cm
(3¹/₂ in); D. base 7.6 cm (3 in); WT. 193.7 gm (6.23 oz)

PROVENANCE: The presenter of this goblet may have
been Joseph B. Lyman, who is listed in the 1857 New
Orleans city directory as an attorney at 13 St. Charles.

Anglo-American Art Museum   72.1
Louisiana State University
Baton Rouge, Louisiana
Gift of the Friends of the Museum

46. Pitcher   ca. 1860-1861

MARKS (on bottom): "HYDE & GOODRICH" incised
in arc, above; "MANUFACTURERS" incised, above;
"WARRANTED/PURE COIN" in scalloped rectangle with pointed ends formed by anthemia, above; "H"
incised; "NEW ORLEANS" incised in complementary arc.

DESCRIPTION: Round, ewer-shaped body on conforming
round, stepped base; applied complex leafy band at
collar; elaborate engine turned bandings encircling
greater portion of body and neck; scrolled, foliate
handle with spurs. "Mrs. J. M. Haden/From/"The
Mess"/Our loss is your gain." engraved within Rococo-
revival cartouche on side of body opposite handle.

MEASUREMENTS: H. 28.0 cm (11¹/₁₆ in); D. base 11.8
cm (4¹¹/₁₆ in); W. 20.1 cm (7¹⁵/₁₆ in); WT. 821.6 gm
(26.42 oz)

LOAN: *Mrs. Albert B. Fay*
Houston, Texas

Although this pitcher was made prior to the
Civil War, the inscription was added shortly thereafter when the present owner's grandfather, J. M.
Hayden, M.D., settled in Galveston, Texas. This
piece was presented to Dr. Hayden's bride by
three of his regular dinner companions, upon her
marriage on January 8, 1868.

Symmetrical engine turnings in zigzag patterns are not common on New Orleans-made silver.

When elaborate engine turned decoration appears
on a piece by Hyde & Goodrich, it is a good indica-
tion that the piece dates from the end of that firm's
activity in 1861. The work would have been done at
the silver manufacturing factory at Bienville and
Derbigny streets. The factory remained intact
through the Civil War and continued to manufacture for A. B. Griswold & Company, the eventual
successor of Hyde & Goodrich, until 1869. A *New
Orleans Times* article, February 11, 1866, de-
scribes this "Mammoth Silverware Factory":

> . . . we are convinced of the ability of
> Messrs. A.B. Griswold & Co., to com-
> pete with the most celebrated manufac-
> turers, in the quality, style and finish of
> their goods, and that through their en-
> terprise wares in their line, may be made
> to order in New Orleans, at a saving of
> the manufacturer's profits, which are
> enormously high. The fact that steam is
> the motive power of their factory re-
> duces the costs of their goods very con-
> siderably, by its labor-saving advan-
> tages, and at the same time enables them
> to execute more accurate workmanship
> with greater dispatch.

47. **Coffee and Tea Service**   **ca. 1855-1861**

MARKS (on bottom of bowl): "HYDE & GOODRICH" incised in arc, above; "H" incised, above; "NEW ORLEANS" incised in complementary arc.

DESCRIPTION: Five-piece service of classical urn shape; repoussé and chased scroll and flower-head cartouches between spiral flutes; cast urn-shaped finials; chased flower sprays and leaves around domed, circular bases; leaf-ornamented swan-neck spouts; double "C"-scroll handles with ivory insulators.

MEASUREMENTS: COFFEE POT: H. 29.3 cm (11½ in); D. base 12.1 cm (4¹³/₁₆ in); W. 28.5 cm (11¼ in); WT. 1026.0 gm (32.99 oz) TEA POT: H. 28.0 cm (11 in); D. base 11.9 cm (4¹¹/₁₆ in); W. 28.9 cm (11³/₈ in); WT. 1054.6 gm (33.91 oz) SUGAR BOWL: H. 24.8 cm (9¾ in); D. base 10.3 cm (4¹/₁₆ in); W. 23.0 cm (9¹/₁₆ in); WT. 789.9 gm (25.40 oz) CREAMER: H. 22.3 cm (8¾ in); D. base 8.8 cm (4⁷/₁₆ in); W. 14.5 cm (5¹¹/₁₆ in); WT. 421.5 gm (13.55 oz) WASTE BOWL: H. 14.0 cm (5½ in); D. lip 14.9 cm (5⁷/₈ in); D. base 10.2 cm (4 in); WT. 407.2 gm (13.09 oz)

LOAN: *Morton's Auction Exchange*
New Orleans, Louisiana

46

48. Covered Cream Jug   ca. 1853-1861

MARKS (on bottom): "HYDE & GOODRICH" incised in
    arc, above: "H" incised, above; "NEW ORLEANS"
    incised in complementary arc.

DESCRIPTION: Baluster-form body chased with morning
    glories; domed lid surmounted by openwork scroll
    handle with heraldic beast head finial; supported on
    applied flared foot with leaf and inverted papyrus
    border; foliate scroll handle. "E M Y" script engraving
    within reserve opposite handle.

MEASUREMENTS: H. 21.6 cm (8½ in); D. base 13.6 cm
    (5³/₈ in); W. 24.1 cm (9½ in); WT. 386.3 gm (12.42 oz)

PROVENANCE: Sotheby Parke Bernet, Inc., New York;
    Sale 4316, lot 337; November 28, 1979.

LOAN: *Dr. and Mrs. A. Brooks Cronan, Jr.*
    Baton Rouge, Louisiana

49. Cake Basket ca. 1853-1861

MARKS (on bottom): "HYDE & GOODRICH" incised
in arc, above; "H" incised, above; "NEW ORLEANS"
incised in complementary arc.

DESCRIPTION: Oval lobed, boat-shaped basket on conforming pedestal base; applied beaded border around
foot; swing handle of four intertwined rope-like strands
of silver. Metal fatigue has caused twenty-eight minor
splits between the lobes on the upper edge of the bowl;
repaired by Christopher A. Hentz.

MEASUREMENTS: H. 27.3 cm (10³/₄ in); L. 33.3 cm
(13¹/₈ in); W. 23.2 cm (9¹/₈ in); WT. 784.7 gm (25.23
oz)

PROVENANCE: Sotheby Parke Bernet, Inc., New York;
Sale 4180, Item 365; November 17, 1978.

Anglo-American Art Museum 79.16.11
Louisiana State University
Baton Rouge, Louisiana
Gift of Mr. and Mrs. William Flores

While numerous advertisements were placed
by Hyde & Goodrich during the 1850s for cake
baskets manufactured by their firm, surviving examples are rare. This Himmel-made basket ranks
with the most attractive of American Victorian
examples of the form. The silversmith demonstrat-
ed his particular skills in manipulating wire strands
of silver into the four intertwined ropes that make
up the handle.

50. Pap Boat   ca. 1853-1861

MARKS (on bottom): "HYDE & GOODRICH" incised; "H" incised.

DESCRIPTION: Oval body with long spout; straight sides tapering slightly from molded lip to flat bottom; "king's" pattern.

MEASUREMENTS: H. 6.5 cm (2⅝ in); L. 16.6 cm (6⁷/₁₆ in); W. 6.5 cm (2⅝ in); WT. 84.9 gm (2.73 oz)

LOAN: *Philip H. Hammerslough Collection Courtesy Wadsworth Atheneum Hartford, Connecticut*

Pap boats, used for feeding infants and invalids, were made both of metal and of ceramics. Primarily an English innovation, they were popular in that country during the eighteenth and the first quarter of the nineteenth centuries. A similar piece made of pottery and called a "sick-cup" was used in New Orleans until fairly late in the nineteenth century. This handsome pap boat, done by Himmel, is a late example and is one of the few extant in silver.

51. Cup   ca. 1853-1861

MARKS (on bottom): "HYDE & GOODRICH" incised in arc, above; "NEW ORLEANS" incised in complementary arc; "H" incised.

DESCRIPTION: Round, baluster-shaped body having lobed lower section; repoussé and chased bird within floral cartouche on upper section; flared lip with applied molding and beading; applied vertical band of rosettes around foot of stepped base; scroll handle. "James M. Vance" engraved in script on side of body.

MEASUREMENTS: H. 12.7 cm (9 in); D. lip 8.0 cm (3¼ in); D. base 6.5 cm (2⁹/₁₆ in); W. 11.2 cm (4⁷/₁₆ in); WT. 143.4 gm (4.61 oz)

PROVENANCE: James Milton Vance was born March 11, 1857, in San Antonio, Texas, son of William Vance. William Vance came from Ireland in 1826 to New York with his father, John Vance, who was a merchant in New York and New Orleans. William Vance went to Texas from New Orleans with General Scott and located in San Antonio. James Milton Vance died February 2, 1930.

LOAN: *Mr. James Vance Gillespie*
San Antonio, Texas

52. Cup   ca. 1853-1861

MARKS (on bottom): "HYDE & GOODRICH" incised in arc, above; "H" incised, above; "NEW ORLEANS" incised in complementary arc.

DESCRIPTION: Round body; molded lip with beading below; straight sides curved at base; applied, flared, molded foot with rosettes flanked by foliate rinceaux beading; repoussé and chased vines, leaves, and flowers forming reserve opposite scroll handle. "From Salome/ to/ Eddie" engraved in script on side.

MEASUREMENTS: H. 9.5 cm (3¹¹/₁₆ in); D. lip 7.4 cm (2⁷/₈ in); D. base 6.0 cm (2⁵/₁₆ in); W. 11.1 cm (4⁵/₁₆ in); WT. 135.7 gm (4.36 oz)

The Historic New Orleans Collection   1978.175.17
New Orleans, Louisiana

53. Pitcher ca. 1853-1861

MARKS (on bottom): "HYDE & GOODRICH" incised in arc, above; "MANUFACTURERS" incised above; "H" incised above; "HYDE & GOODRICH" incised in arc, upside down.

DESCRIPTION: Bulbous pear-shaped body with molded lip and spout; repoussé and chased body of scrolling foliage and flowers; "C"-scroll cartouches on either side of body; naturalistic twig-like handle with flower heads and leaves; flared, molded circular foot. "Presented/to/James Herron, Esqr./Civil Engineer/ by the/Citizens of Warrington and Woolsey, as a testimonial of/their high estimation of the public benefit done the Country by his/Engineering ability and perserverance in the eminently/successful construction of the PERMANENT GRANITE WHARF/and other improvements, and also for his integrity, just,/and impartial discharge of his official duties as Engineer/in Chief of Navy Yard/Pensacola." engraved in script in one cartouche; "Let him bear the palm/Who hath deserved it." engraved in script in other.

MEASUREMENTS: H. 20.9 cm (8¼ in); D. base 13.5 cm (5⁵/₁₆ in); W. 24.8 cm (9¾ in); WT. 962.1 gm (30.93 oz)

PROVENANCE: The development of the two Florida communities of Warrington and Woolsey occurred in the late 1820s and early 1830s. Warrington bordered the old Navy Yard to the west, and Woolsey (much smaller) to the east. Both communities were abandoned in the twentieth century when the Navy Yard became the Pensacola Naval Air Station. Warrington was re-established across the lagoon. James Herron sent plans and estimates to the U.S. Secretary of the Navy for the construction of a permanent wharf and dry dock at Pensacola. The report is dated February 19, 1844. By 1849, the construction of the dry dock had gotten under way with an appropriation of almost one million dollars. In addition to the dry dock a three hundred twenty foot granite wharf was under construction. (Information provided by Mr. Gordon N. Simons, Curator, Pensacola Historical Museum, Pensacola, Florida.)

Anglo-American Art Museum 80.2.3
Louisiana State University
Baton Rouge, Louisiana
Gift of Dr. and Mrs. A. Brooks Cronan, Jr.

This presentation pitcher was made by Himmel after his association with Hyde & Goodrich began in 1853. It is somewhat curious that the citizens of Warrington and Woolsey would purchase the piece in New Orleans, and thus by-pass the excellent silversmiths in nearby Mobile, Alabama.

The pitcher is stylistically similar to the earlier Küchler & Himmel pitcher (cat. no. 36) and the Küchler pitcher (cat. no. 40).

54. Pitcher   ca. 1853-1861

MARKS (on bottom): "HYDE & GOODRICH" incised in arc, above; "H" incised, above; "NEW ORLEANS" incised in complementary arc.

DESCRIPTION: Bulbous pear-shaped body with restrained repoussé and chased grapevine, leaves, and grape clusters forming reserve on either side; applied molding at lip with elaborate applied shell spout; applied flared foot of running curule-and-cross banding; naturalistic scroll handle. "BADGETT" engraved in script on body.

MEASUREMENTS: H. 24.8 cm (9³⁄₄ in); D. base 12.5 cm (4¹⁵⁄₁₆ in); W. 24.1 cm (9¹⁄₂ in); WT. 1002.4 gm (32.22 oz)

LOAN: *Morton's Auction Exchange*
New Orleans, Louisiana

Elements of Adolphe Himmel's pitcher are very similar to those of a silver chinoiserie pitcher retailed by Tiffany, Young & Ellis of New York, and made about 1850 (illustrated in Carpenter, *Tiffany Silver*, p. 181). The handle and spout are almost identical. Another pitcher, retailed by Lincoln and Foss, Boston, about 1851, is similar in the treatment of the spout and body (illustrated in Gourley, *The New England Silversmith*, fig. 76). Even though such prototypes were not actually brought to New Orleans from the northeast, local silversmiths were aware of the styles current in New York and Boston. Notwithstanding the obvious borrowings, Himmel exhibited true individuality and facility in executing his own hand-chased decoration on this and similar pitchers (cat. nos. 36, 40, 53).

This pitcher was part of a set belonging to the Badgett family and made by Himmel for Hyde & Goodrich. The set also included four matched beakers also bearing the engraved "BADGETT" name. Two of the beakers are now owned by the Louisiana State Museum, New Orleans.

55. Tureen and Ladle   ca. 1861-1877

MARKS (on bottom of tureen): "A.H./N.O." incised, above; "WARRANTED/PURE COIN" in scalloped rectangular cartouche with pointed ends formed by anthemia.

DESCRIPTION: TUREEN: Rococo-revival oval body with bombé sides; raised on conforming oval foot; everted rim and foot edge bordered in heavy naturalistic cast grapevines, grape clusters, and leaves; repoussé and chased grapevine motif stemming from naturalistic intertwined twig handles on domed lid and on body. LADLE: Elaborately decorated single-faced handle; oval bowl with gilded interior. "C.A.F. Rondeau" engraved in Gothic lettering on side of tureen.

MEASUREMENTS: TUREEN: H. 29.2 cm (11¾ in); L. 39.4 cm (15½ in); W. 25.4 cm (10 in); WT. 1569.1 gm (50.45 oz) LADLE: L. 39.4 cm (15½ in); D. bowl 12.3 cm (4⅞ in); WT. 453.9 gm (14.59 oz)

PROVENANCE: Charles Augustus Frederick Rondeau was a prominent banker in New Orleans prior to the Civil War. In 1851, he married Miss Jane Arkinstall. He appears to have moved from New Orleans in the late 1850s. Mrs. Rondeau died at her home in Market Drayton, Shropshire, England, in 1892, at age seventy-five.

Anglo-American Art Museum 78.2.1a, b-2
Louisiana State University
Baton Rouge, Louisiana
Gift of Dr. and Mrs. A. Brooks Cronan, Jr.

Although not made until after 1861, this tureen and ladle are in the high Rococo-revival style, with ornamentation relating closely to the Badgett family pitcher made by Himmel before the Civil War (cat. no. 54). All dated pieces bearing the same Himmel mark were made in the 1870s, following the A. B. Griswold & Co.–Himmel dissolution in 1869. The late date for a work in Rococo-revival makes the tureen a classic example of the retarditaire nature of much of the South's decorative arts and shows how a long-established decorative style can be further refined by a master silversmith even after many years of repeated application.

56. Cup   ca. 1866-1877

MARK (on bottom): "A. HIMMEL./COIN." incised.

DESCRIPTION: Round body with tapered, angular sides; recessed center portion with chased oval cartouche between flowers and leaves and opposite angular handle; molded lip with beading below; applied guilloche border on molded base. "BE/von/LM" engraved in script on side of body.

MEASUREMENTS: H. 7.9 cm (3⅛ in); D. lip 6.0 cm (2⅜ in); D. base 7.0 cm (2¾ in); W. 8.1 cm (3³/₁₆ in); WT. 106.0 gm (3.40 oz)

Anglo-American Art Museum 79.35
Louisiana State University
Baton Rouge, Louisiana
Gift of the Friends of the Museum

57. Cup   ca. 1870

MARKS (on bottom): "A.H." incised, above; "NEW ORLEANS." incised.

DESCRIPTION: Cylindrical cup; applied, gadrooned border at lip and around upper part of high, molded base; repoussé and chased flower sprays with round punch-work ground within pendentives formed by four arched divisions around body; egg-and-dart border edged with beading on applied vertical foot. "Allen Melhle,/From his Mother,/Aug. 21ˢᵗ 1870" engraved in script on body opposite handle.

MEASUREMENTS: H. 8.3 cm (3¼ in); D. lip 6.4 cm (2½ in); D. base 7.4 cm (2⅞ in); W. 9.4 cm (3¹¹/₁₆ in); WT. 120.8 gm (3.88 oz)

The Historic New Orleans Collection 1978.175.15
New Orleans, Louisiana

58. Cup and Saucer   ca. 1873

MARKS (on bottom of cup only): "A.H." incised, above; "NEW ORLEANS" incised, smaller than above.

DESCRIPTION: CUP: Inverted pear-shaped body; finely gadrooned flared lip with beading below; restrained repoussé and chased scrolls, waves, foliage, and flowers forming cartouche opposite flat, curved handle with thumbpiece; circular base with applied molding and gadrooned foot. SAUCER: Conforming to cup base; engraved stylized leaves around center. "R.F. & E.F./ to/J. & A.N./Nov. 7th 1873" engraved in script on body of cup.

MEASUREMENTS: CUP: H. 8.6 cm (3³/₈ in); D. lip 9.5 cm (3³/₄ in); D. base 6.0 cm (2³/₈ in); WT. 127.7 gm (4.11 oz) SAUCER: H. 1.6 cm (⁵/₈ in); D. 12.7 cm (5 in); WT. 95.7 gm (3.08 oz)

The Historic New Orleans Collection   1979.371 a, b
New Orleans, Louisiana

The precise use of this silver cup and saucer and those by A. B. Griswold (cat. no.59) and by Gregor & Wilson (cat. no. 111) is unknown. None of the cups have heat insulators. Although cold beverages could have been served in this type of cup and saucer, they were more probably presentation pieces or special gifts.

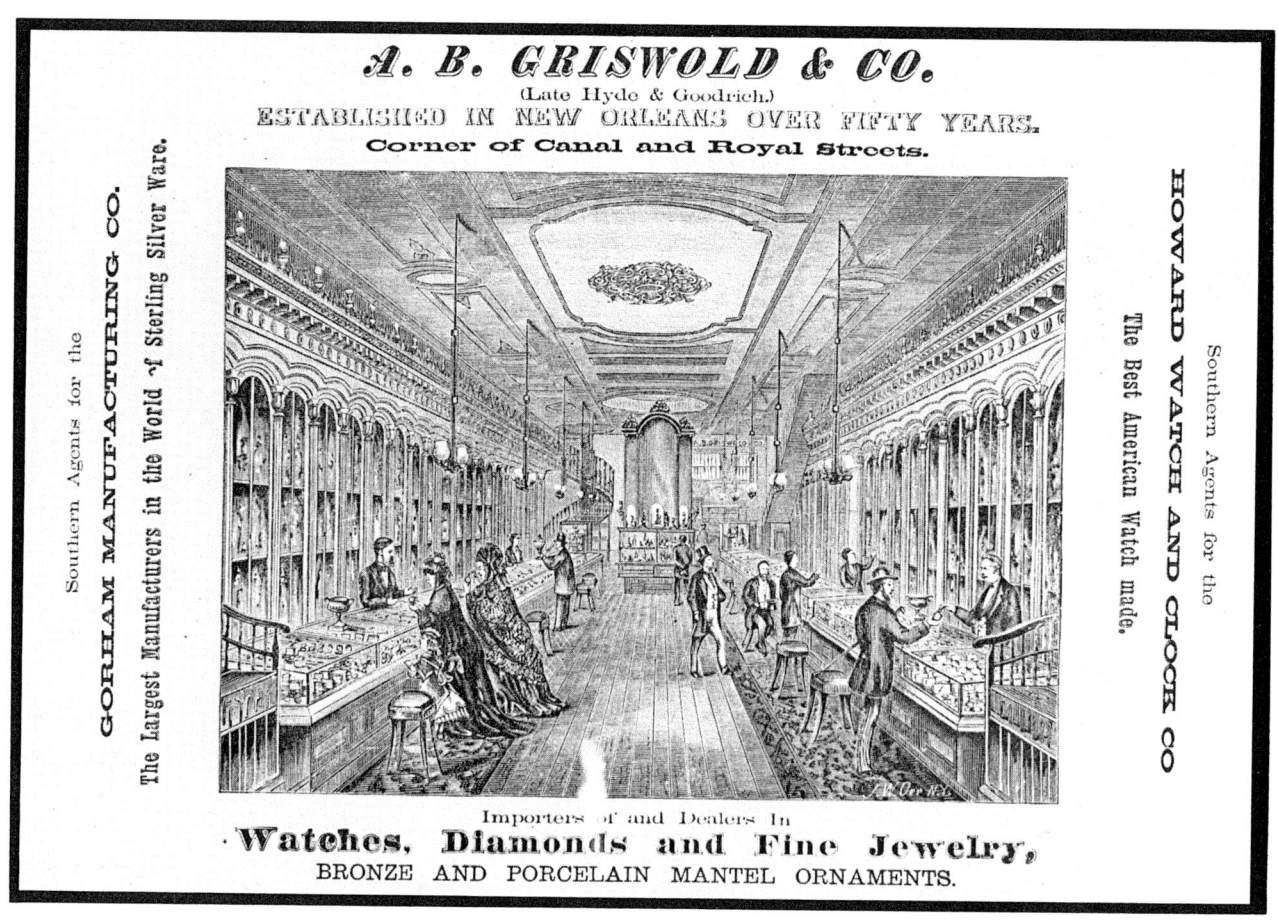

A. B. Griswold & Co. advertisement. Jewell, Edwin L. *Jewell's Crescent City Illustrated.* New Orleans, 1873. (The Historic New Orleans Collection)

A. B. GRISWOLD & CO.

Thomas, Griswold & Co., successor of Hyde & Goodrich, was compelled to change the firm name following the death of Henry Thomas, Jr., in 1864. The new title of the firm, A. B. Griswold & Co., was not adopted until 1865.

Adolphe Himmel, chief silversmith of Hyde & Goodrich, and of Thomas, Griswold & Co., continued in that capacity with A.B. Griswold & Co. until about 1869. After that time A. B. Griswold & Co. was primarily an importer, occasionally relying on Himmel for specialty pieces.

A. B. Griswold operated as a partnership until 1906; it included A. B. Griswold, William McLeary Goodrich, and Henry Ginder. Following the death of A. B. Griswold in 1877, Mrs. Fanny Newman Griswold, widow of A.B. Griswold, and their son, George Palfrey Griswold, were partners in the firm. There were a multitude of other partners with minor interests.

In 1906 the firm was incorporated under the title of A.B. Griswold & Co., Ltd. The share-holders were: Henry Ginder, 996 shares; and, George Palfrey Griswold, Arthur Griswold Palfrey, Edgar L. Roane, and William B. Young, one share each. By 1922, at the age of ninety, Henry Ginder died and the other shareholders were growing old. In January of 1924, A. B. Griswold & Co., Ltd., sold out to Hausmann's although the business did not close down immediately.

The purchase of A.B. Griswold & Co. by Hausmann's completed the circle by uniting the successor of Hyde & Goodrich with the successor of Adolphe Himmel.

A. B. Griswold & Co. was the New Orleans agent for The Gorham Manufacturing Company, of Providence, Rhode Island. Organized as a corporation in 1865, Gorham adopted the sterling standard in 1868. The Gorham Company was among the first to introduce mass production to the handcrafting of silver.

59. Cup and Saucer ca. 1865-1877

MARKS (on bottom of saucer): "A. B. GRISWOLD & CO./N.O.-H" incised.

DESCRIPTION: CUP: Cone-shaped body on simple, molded foot; raised band encircling cup with cast, applied bust of child looking left within cartouche of scrolls, punchwork, and foliate motifs. SAUCER: Round, molded saucer with applied vertical foot of guilloche banding. "J. Israel" engraved on outer edge of handle; "M" engraved on right side of handle.

MEASUREMENTS: CUP: H. 6.6 cm (2⅝ in); D. lip 6.6 cm (2⅝ in); D. base 3.0 cm (1³/₁₆ in); W. 8.1 cm (3³/₁₆ in); WT. 99.9 gm (3.21 oz) SAUCER: H. 1.9 cm (¾ in); D. 11.4 cm (4½ in); WT. 73.0 gm (2.35 oz)

Anglo-American Art Museum 68.6.32 a,b
Louisiana State University
Baton Rouge, Louisiana
Gift of Mrs. H. Payne Breazeale, Sr.

A. B. Griswold & Co. store, corner of Canal and Royal Streets. "Touro Buildings, Canal Street," undated wood engraving. (The Historic New Orleans Collection 1959.157.5)

60. Medal   ca. 1878

MARKS (on back of ribbon banner): "A.B.G. & Co." incised in arc, above; "N.O." incised.

DESCRIPTION: Gold medal; ribbon banner attached by gold link to "HA" cipher monogram attached by gold link to circular disc with bright-cut engraving. "1878" engraved on ribbon banner; "Presented to/George Ferry/By the/Howard Association." engraved on obverse of disc; "For faithful service" engraved on reverse of disc.

MEASUREMENTS: L. 6.8 cm (2¹¹/₁₆ in); W. 3.3 cm (1⁵/₁₆ in); WT. 10.4 gm (.33 oz)

PROVENANCE: The Howard Association was named for John Howard, a noted New Orleans philanthropist. Founded in 1837, the Association paid doctors to treat the poor and destitute during the yellow fever epidemics. Following the yellow fever epidemic in Shreveport, Louisiana, in 1874, it commissioned gold medals from A. B. Griswold & Co. Undoubtedly, Henry Ginder, one-time president of the Association and a partner in A. B. Griswold & Co., arranged for these medals from his firm. Following the devastating epidemic in 1878, the Howard Association again presented gold medals for faithful service.

The Historic New Orleans Collection   1978.51.3a
New Orleans, Louisiana

61. Bell   ca. 1899

MARKS (lower outer molding of bell): "A. B. GRISWOLD & CO." incised to the right of; pseudo-hallmarks of Gorham Manufacturing Company of Providence, Rhode Island, followed by; "STERLI-" incised.

DESCRIPTION: Round body; handle formed by two upright dolphins holding shell in mouths; convex moldings encircling top above running dolphin banding; plain, broad mid-band decorated with Great Seal of the United States Navy in bas relief, surrounded by circular border and encircled by laurel wreath with ribbons. Broad baseband with cotton bolls and foliage between crossed sugarcane stalks in bas relief above smaller foliate and arch band. "U.S.S. NEW ORLE" engraved on border (imperfectly cast).

MEASUREMENTS: H. 7.0 cm (2³/₄ in); D. base 5.8 cm (2⁵/₁₆ in); WT. 102.0 gm (3.28 oz)

PROVENANCE: A. B. Griswold & Co. of New Orleans secured the honor of placing the silver service order for the cruiser *U.S.S. New Orleans*. The order was placed with the Gorham Manufacturing Company of Providence, Rhode Island, and included punch bowl, waiter, twenty-four goblets, and one pair of comports fourteen inches in diameter. Gorham also supplied to A. B. Griswold & Co. the design for the ship's bell. However, since Gorham's price for making the bell was too costly, it was manufactured in New Orleans by M. Scooler and Co. The ship was presented with the silver service and bell on May 24, 1899. This bell is a souvenir version of the ship's bell.

Anglo-American Art Museum   79.5
Louisiana State University
Baton Rouge, Louisiana
Gift of the Friends of the Museum

The small souvenir bell was made by Gorham in Providence, Rhode Island, and retailed in New Orleans through A. B. Griswold & Co. It is based on the design for the ship's bell, also provided by Gorham.

T. HAUSMANN & SONS

Henry Hausmann arrived in New Orleans in 1870. Allegedly, Hausmann and an old friend formed the jewelry partnership of Lautenschlaeger and Hausmann. The existence of this partnership cannot be verified.

By 1874, Henry Hausmann was working as a jeweler at Adolphe Himmel's. Hausmann then appears to have been working at an adjacent location with some sort of business relationship with Himmel. Following Himmel's death in 1877, Hausmann took over the business, advertising that he would continue to manufacture silverware, plated ware, headlights for locomotives and steamboats, saddler's brass, silver letters, and findings. Hausmann died in 1878, during the yellow fever epidemic, leaving behind a widow and two small sons.

His widow, Theresa Hausmann, continued to operate the business under the name of H. Hausmann until 1880. From 1881 to 1889, with fifteen male assistants, she operated the firm under her own name, T. Hausmann. Her eldest son, Louis, was admitted to the firm, which became T. Hausmann & Son from 1890 until 1893. In 1894 the title was again changed to reflect the admission of the younger son, Gabriel, more frequently known as "Gabe." The business flourished from 1894 to 1907, when the firm was incorporated as T. Hausmann & Sons, Ltd. By the early 1920s, the name had been shortened to simply Hausmann's. Hausmann's bought out A. B. Griswold & Co., Ltd., in 1924. Unfortunately Mrs. Theresa Hausmann died within a few weeks of the purchase. As the successor of A. Himmel, Hausmann's had absorbed A.B. Griswold & Co., the successor of Hyde & Goodrich.

The early Hausmann silver is in fact a continuation of the silver produced by Himmel. Otherwise identical "fiddle thread" forks and spoons are frequently found with some pieces bearing Himmel's "A.H." while others contain Hausmann's "H.H." After the death of Henry Hausmann, the firm continued to manufacture silver, but retailed its more complex pieces from northwestern producers. For years following the closing of Griswold's, Hausmann's was the preferred "old-line" establishment.

Hausmann's store, 135 Baronne Street. Ca. 1915 photograph by Charles L. Franck. (The Historic New Orleans Collection 1979.89)

In polite society in the nineteenth and early twentieth centuries, suspenders were not customarily seen in public gatherings of ladies and gentlemen. They would have been covered by waistcoats and jackets. In Louisiana's warm, humid climate, jackets and waistcoats could be removed during certain all-male functions, where monogrammed Hausmann suspender buckles would have been a nice accoutrement for the well-dressed gentleman. Doubtless, some of these handsome buckles were originally owned by New Orleans's less well-bred, but showy, men such as gamblers and owners of sporting houses.

T. Hausmann & Son advertised eight styles of suspender buckles, the prices of which increased with more complicated decoration and with gold replacing some silver parts.

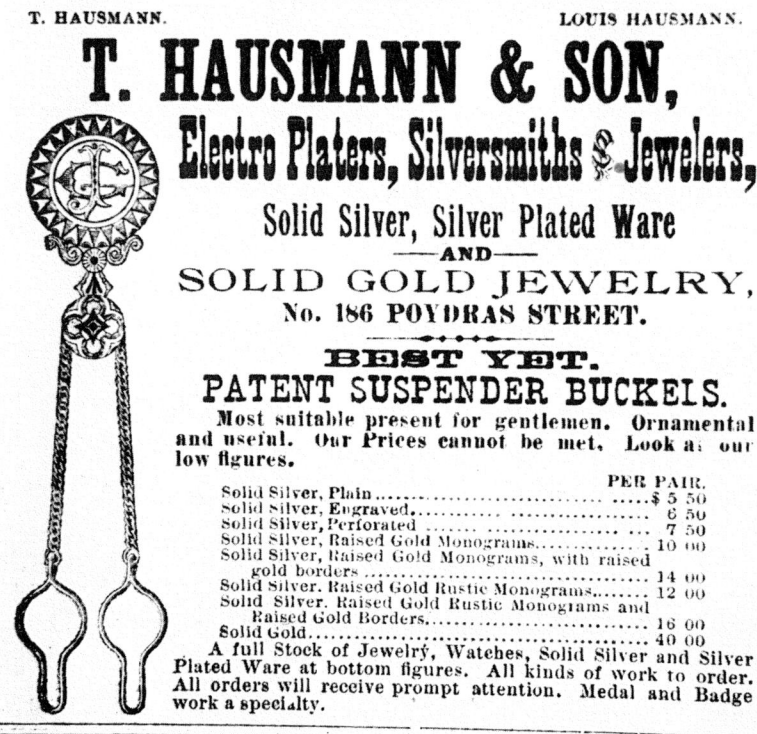

T. Hausmann & Son advertisement. *Soards' New Orleans Directory*. New Orleans: L. Soards, 1891. (The Historic New Orleans Collection)

62. Suspender Buckles   ca. 1894-1907

MARKS (on back of clips): "T. HAUSMANN & SONS" incised in arc, above; "STERLING" incised, above; "N.O." incised, above; "LA" incised within arc.

DESCRIPTION: Pulley-type apparatus on each with wooden core on pivot attached to circular border containing pierced Gothic-revival cipher monogram "H R C"; engraved scrolls and beading; chains terminating in button loops; hinged clips on backs for holding suspender straps.

MEASUREMENTS: L. each 15.8 cm (6¼ in); W. each 3.8 cm (1½ in); WTS. 30.4 gm (.98 oz); 29.5 gm (.95 oz)

*The Historic New Orleans Collection   1978.175.8.1-2
New Orleans, Louisiana*

63. Suspender Buckles   ca. 1894-1907

MARK (on back of clips): "T. HAUSMANN & SONS" incised.

DESCRIPTION: Pulley-type apparatus on each with wooden core on pivot attached to circular frame containing pierced cipher gold monogram "BR"; bright-cut engraving; chain terminating in button loops; hinged clip on back for holding suspender straps.

MEASUREMENTS: L. each 16.5 cm (6½ in); W. each 4.2 cm (1⅝ in); WTS. 32.4 gm (1.04 oz); 31.1 gm (1.00 oz)

*The Historic New Orleans Collection   1979.375.1-2
New Orleans, Louisiana*

61

PART II

The candlesticks, candle snuffer and tray, and the salts were all made for Pierre Denis de La Ronde (1762-1824), a prominent official during the Spanish regime in Louisiana. De La Ronde fought with Bernardo de Galvez in West Florida, was military commandant of St. Bernard Parish, Louisiana, was a member of the Cabildo from 1798 to 1803, and served as a colonel under Andrew Jackson in the Battle of New Orleans. His home, Versailles Plantation, located along the Mississippi River in St. Bernard Parish, was occupied by the British and used as a hospital during the battle.

These silver articles were used at his home. The engraving on them was not his family coat of arms, but an insignia with which he marked his personal belongings.

Imported French silver pieces such as these served as prototypes for French emigrant and American silversmiths—particularly Simon Chaudron, Fletcher and Gardiner, and Anthony Rasch.

Pierre Denis de La Ronde. Undated wood engraving by Lossing & Barrit. Lossing, Benson J. *The Pictorial Field-Book of the War of 1812.* New York: Harper & Brothers, 1869. (The Historic New Orleans Collection)

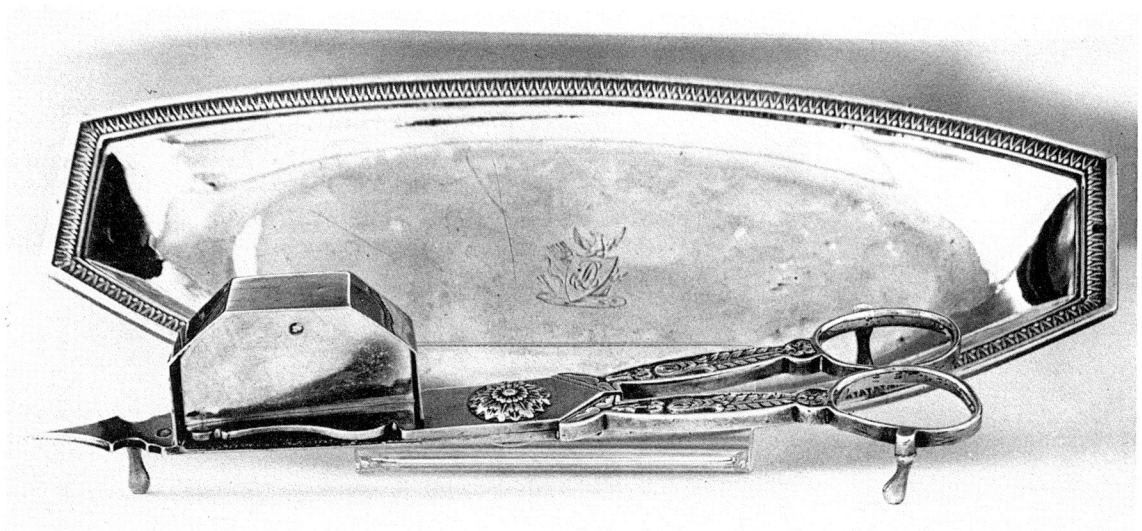

64. Snuffer and Tray   ca. 1803-1819

MARKS (on lid and handles of snuffer, and on rims of tray): Silver assay marks for Paris, first standard, 1803-1819. Makers' marks unidentified.

DESCRIPTION: SNUFFER: Scissor-form with foliate ornamented handles and oval thumbholes; flat, shaped stems, one with shaped, pointed end, for pan and plate; short support at end and on each thumbhole. TRAY: Oval-shaped body with angular ends; flat bottom with up curved sides; palmette, ball, and string border around edge. De La Ronde family crest engraved in center.

MEASUREMENTS: SNUFFER: L. 17.5 cm (6 7/8 in); W. 5.5 cm (2 1/8 in); WT. 105.8 gm (3.40 oz) TRAY: L. 20.7 cm (8 1/8 in); W. 9.6 cm (3 3/4 in); WT. 127.6 gm (4.10 oz)

The Historic New Orleans Collection 1977.308.4-5
New Orleans, Louisiana
Gift of Mr. James A. Stouse

65. Salt Frame with Crystal Liner ca. 1803-1819

MARKS (on circular frame): Silver assay marks for Paris, first standard, 1803-1819. Maker unidentified.

DESCRIPTION: Circular frame with applied, palmette, ball, and string banding at flared rim; three straight legs with ball feet and with applied eagle, wings spread; arched stretchers between legs. Crystal liner is replacement.

MEASUREMENTS: H. 5.9 cm (2⁵⁄₁₆ in); D. 7.7 cm (3 in); WT. 64.2 gm (2.06 oz)

The Historic New Orleans Collection   1978.246.1.2a,b
New Orleans, Louisiana
Gift of Mr. James A. Stouse

66. Pair of Candlesticks ca. 1803-1819

MARKS (on base, shaft, and nozzle of each): Silver assay marks for Paris, first standard, 1803-1819. Makers' marks unidentified.

DESCRIPTION: French Empire hexagonal shafts each tapered from three Egyptian female forms supporting urn-shaped nozzle with bobeche to three monopode supports; circular, molded bases with vertical feet; classical ornamentation. "DL" engraved in script cipher in crest on flat, upper surface of base.

MEASUREMENTS: H. each 28.0 cm (11 in); D. base each 13.4 cm (5¼ in); WTS. 533.1 gm (17.14 oz); 536.1 gm (17.24 oz)

The Historic New Orleans Collection   1977.308.6.1-2
New Orleans, Louisiana
Gift of Mr. James A. Stouse

JEAN-NOEL DELARUE

Jean-Noel Delarue was born in Baccalans, a suburb of Bordeaux, France, in 1776. He first came to New Orleans about 1802, but traveled back and forth to his native land. In 1810 he publicized his recent return from France with an elegant assortment of jewelry from Paris. He moved his store in 1813 from Royal Street to Chartres Street, and advertised that he would continue to fabricate and sell all kinds of work including coffee pots, forks, and spoons. Eleven years later he returned to Royal Street, this time at #138, next to Mr. Ducatel. Again he advertised his skills, along with his desire to purchase old articles of gold and silver. He died in New Orleans in 1842.

Delarue was the most prolific New Orleans silversmith of the early nineteenth century. Generally pieces bearing the Delarue marks conform to contemporary French styles, with which he was undoubtedly familiar.

67. Beaker ca. 1824

MARK (on bottom): "De/Larue" script letters in oval.

DESCRIPTION: Raised cylindrical body; flared lip; flat bottom. "Numa Vignie" engraved in script on side.

MEASUREMENTS: H. 7.7 cm (3 in)

PROVENANCE: According to family history, the beaker was presented to Daniel Lewis Gibbens by fellow members of the General Court of Massachusetts upon his retirement in 1824 or 1825. It descended in his family to the present owner. Gibbens kept a fancy grocery store in Boston and, again according to family history, imported many items from New Orleans. Further family connections with New Orleans existed through one of Daniel Gibbens's sons, a physician who lived in that city.

LOAN: *Private Collection*

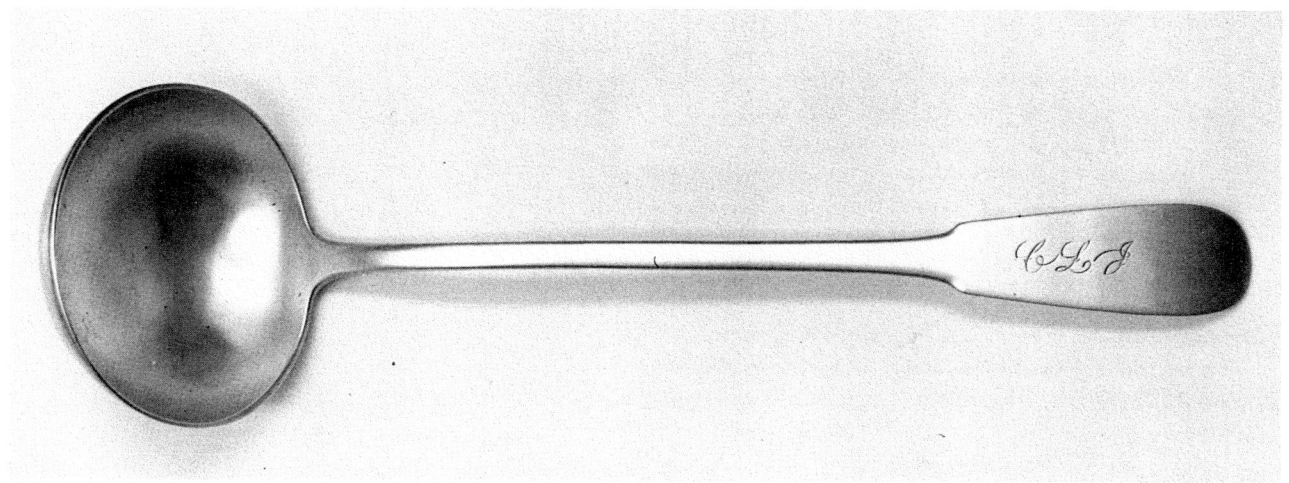

68. Ladle ca. 1820-1830

MARKS (on back of handle): "De/Larue" script letters in oval flanked by; bees in octagonal cartouches.

DESCRIPTION: "Fiddle" handle, down curved end, with midrib, tapered to circular bowl with double drop on back at juncture with handle. "CLJ" engraved on upper face of handle.

MEASUREMENTS: L. 33.7 cm (13¼ in); D. bowl 9.5 cm (3¾ in); WT. 222.4 gm (7.15 oz)

Anglo-American Art Museum 77.3.3
Louisiana State University
Baton Rouge, Louisiana
Gift of the Friends of the Museum

69. Two Soup Spoons and Two Forks ca. 1820-1835

MARK: "Delarue" script, in oval; flanked by bees in circular cartouches (on back of handle).

DESCRIPTION: "Fiddle" handles, up curved ends with midrib, tapered to pointed oval bowls of spoons or long tines of forks. "C.D." engraved in block letters on upper back of handles.

MEASUREMENTS: SOUP SPOONS: L. each 20.9 cm (8¼ in); WTS. 73.1 gm (2.35 oz); 72.9 gm (2.34 oz) FORKS: L. each 20.5 (8⅛ in); WTS. 80.5 gm (2.59 oz); 82.1 gm (2.64 oz)

Anglo-American Art Museum 80.3.1-4
Louisiana State University
Baton Rouge, Louisiana
Gift of Katherine H. Long and the
Friends of the Museum

The majority of surviving flatware sets in the French "fiddle" back style, made by Jean Delarue and also by a member of the Lamothe family, consist of large spoons and forks, but no teaspoons. The large spoons seem to have taken the place of teaspoons and were used for both soups and desserts. While there are records as far back as the mid-eighteenth century of well-to-do Louisianians having sumptuous sets of silver, crystal, and china, that seems to have been the exception rather than the rule. One distinguished early nineteenth-century visitor from New York noted the lack of large place settings of flatware. John Pintard, who became one of the founders of the New-York Historical Society in 1804, lived in New Orleans during 1801. In one of his letters he observed, ". . . there is no display of plate beyond the spoon and fork— and as to porcelain or chrystal [sic] services they are totally unknown . . ." (Editor David Lee Sterling: "New Orleans 1801: An Account by John Pintard," *The Louisiana Historical Quarterly*, July 1951, vol. 34, no. 3, p. 225).

At the time of Pintard's visit New Orleans was still a small town. Perhaps this "American" was not invited to the best homes of the affluent Creoles, where he might have seen more luxurious table settings. Also, it is to be noted that the French, in general, have not always shared the penchant peculiar to the British and the Americans for having a special utensil for every function of dining. Much later in the century, a more heterogeneous and international New Orleans populace indulged in that Victorian propensity.

PIERRE LAMOTHE

Relatively little is known of Pierre Lamothe, master silversmith. He lived for a time in St. Marc, Santo Domingo, where he married Marie Couvertié, a native of Port-au-Prince, daughter of Jean Couvertié and Marie Anne Brandy Couvertié. Because of the slave uprisings, the family fled from Santo Domingo to Santiago de Cuba, about 1803. The expulsion of the French from Cuba forced the withdrawal of Pierre and his immediate family to New Orleans by 1810. His father-in-law accompanied them, but died a year later, at age seventy-three.

In 1813, Lamothe advertised that he was moving his shop to the corner of St. Louis and Royal Streets. It is also known that during the Battle of New Orleans in January, 1815, he served as a private in Plauché's Battalion of Louisiana Militia.

By 1821, with his son Jean-Marie Lamothe, Pierre was working under the name of Lamothe *et fils,* when they moved their shop to Royal Street between St. Ann and Dumaine. Pierre Lamothe is last listed in the 1823 city directory. Thereafter the business was carried on by his two sons, Jean-Marie Lamothe and Jean-Baptiste Lamothe.

Pierre Lamothe is related to the largest family of silversmiths in New Orleans. Among the silversmiths he was related to were: his father-in-law, Jean Couvertié; his brothers-in-law, Jean-Baptiste Couvertié and Louis Gabriel Couvertié; his two surviving sons, Jean-Marie Lamothe and Jean-Baptiste Lamothe; at least one grandson, Michel Meilleur, Jr.; and several nephews, including Jean-Baptiste and Emile Couvertié.

Surviving examples of Pierre Lamothe's silver conform to traditional standards of French colonial silver, very simple and very heavy.

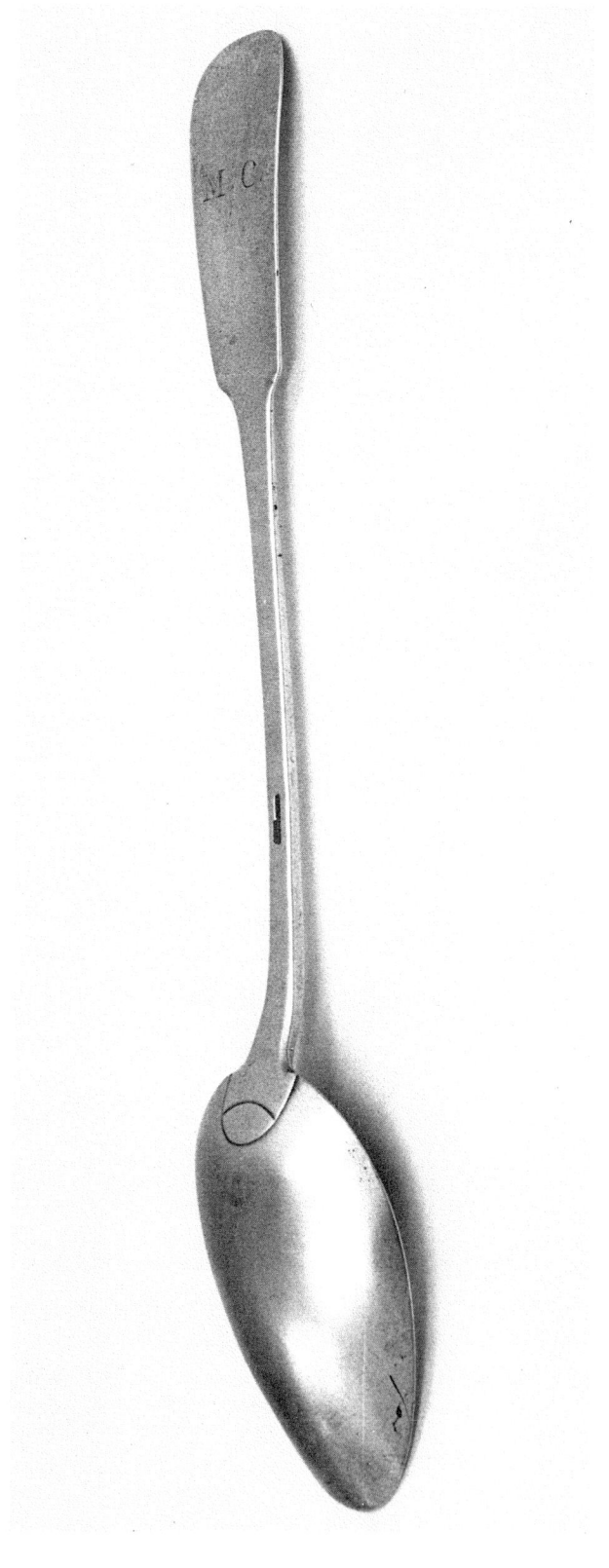

70. Gravy or Stew Spoon   ca. 1810-1823

MARK (on back of handle): "P. Lamothe" script letters in cartouche.

DESCRIPTION: "Fiddle" handle, up curved end with midrib; long straight tapered shank; oval bowl with double drop on back at juncture with handle. "MC" engraved on back of handle.

MEASUREMENTS: L. 39.4 cm (15½ in); WT. 272.4 gm (8.76 oz)

LOAN: *Private Collection*

This spoon is unusually large even for the generally big French-style pieces. It is greater in size than the ladle (cat. no. 71), up to now the largest known utensil by P. Lamothe.

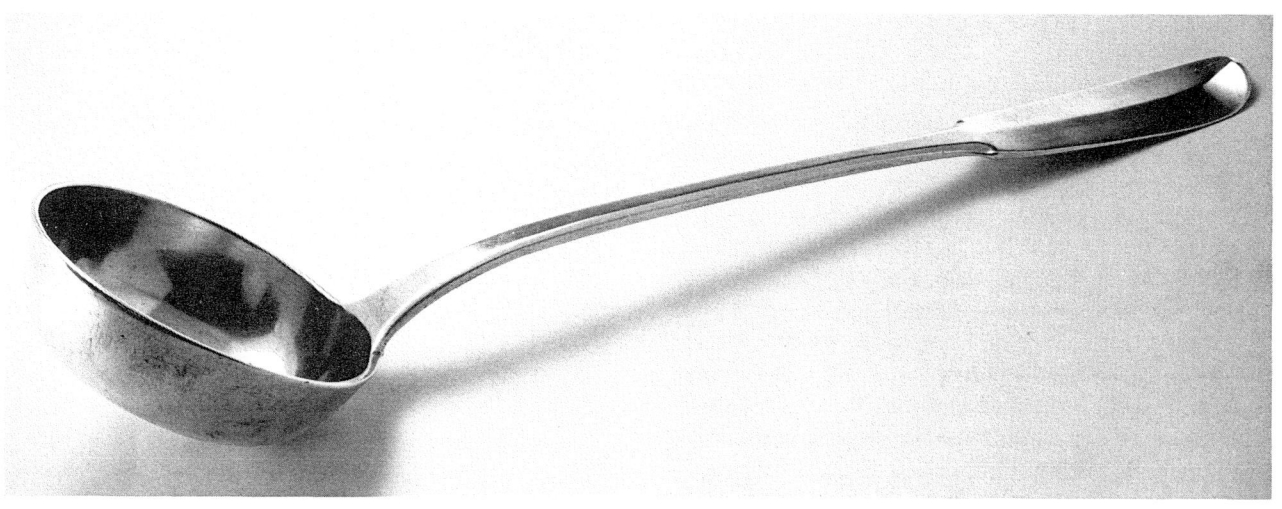

71. Ladle   ca. 1810-1823

MARK (on back of handle): "P. Lamothe" script letters in cartouche.

DESCRIPTION: "Fiddle" handle, up curved end with mid-rib, long tapered shank; round, broad, flat bowl.

MEASUREMENTS: L. 34.9 cm (13³/₄ in); D. bowl 9.4 cm (3¹¹/₁₆ in); WT. 268.0 gm (8.62 oz.)

LOAN: *The Museum of Fine Arts   B.71.93*
Bayou Bend Collection
Houston, Texas

72. Tongs   ca. 1810-1823

MARK (on inside of arm): "P. Lamothe" script letters in conforming cartouche.

DESCRIPTION: Two "fiddle" handles terminating in acorn-shaped grips.

MEASUREMENTS: L. 17.5 cm (7 in); W. 6.4 cm (2¹/₂ in); WT. 67.7 gm (2.18 oz)

Anglo-American Art Museum   79.16.1
Louisiana State University
Baton Rouge, Louisiana
Gift of Dr. and Mrs. A. Brooks Cronan, Jr.

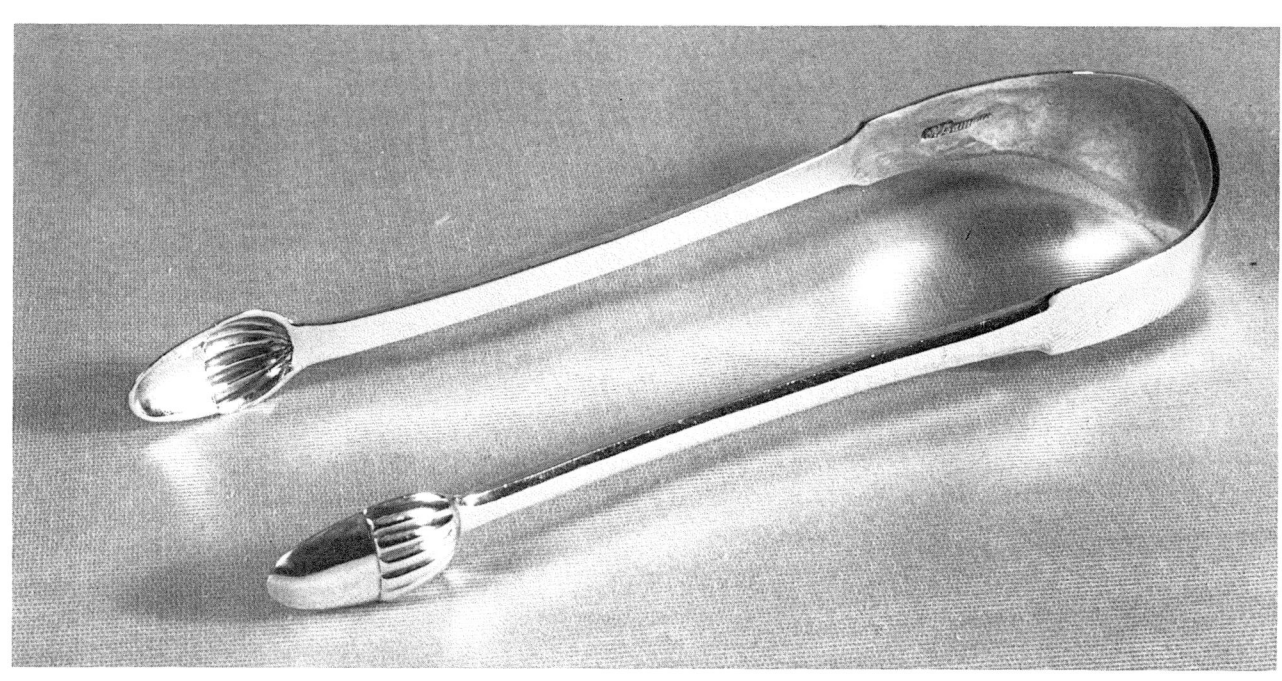

LOUIS GABRIEL COUVERTIÉ

Louis Gabriel Couvertié was born in St. Marc, Santo Domingo, ca. 1779. He was the son of Jean and Marie Anne Brandy Couvertié, and the brother of Marie Couvertié, wife of Pierre Lamothe. He was married to Marguerite Kunt, also a native of St. Marc. In 1803, uprisings caused the entire family to flee to Santiago de Cuba. About 1809, when the French-speaking people were expelled from Cuba, Louis and his family separated from the Lamothe branch and left for Baltimore. He arrived in New Orleans sometime in 1814, and served as a sergeant in Plauché's Battalion, Louisiana Militia, during the Battle of New Orleans.

Louis Gabriel Couvertié died in New Orleans in 1844 and was buried in the family tomb in St. Louis Cemetery #2. His wife died in 1865.

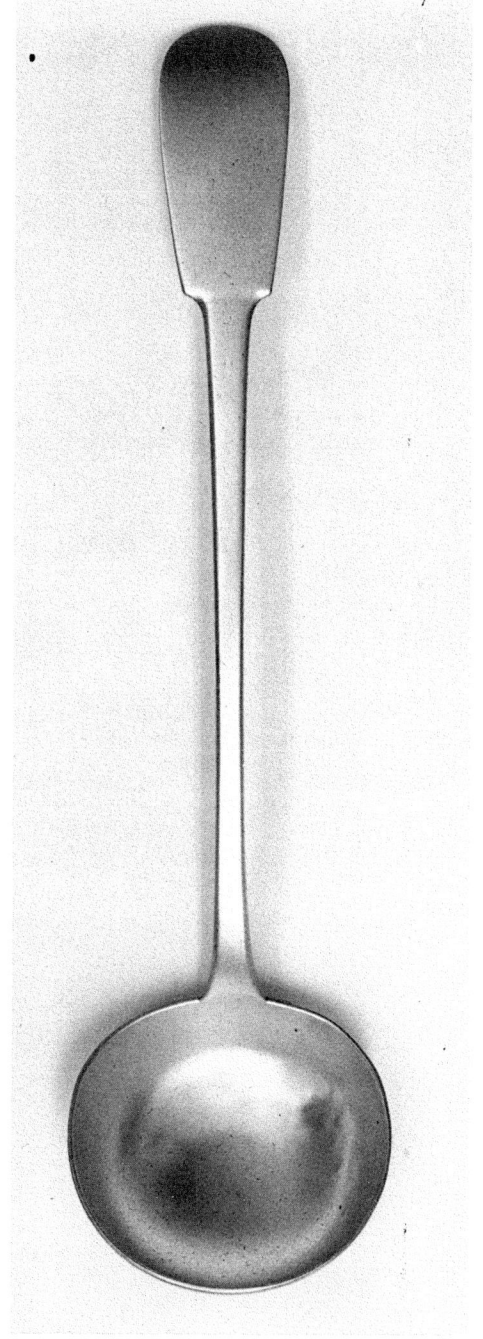

73.　Ladle　ca. 1815-1830

MARK (on back of handle): "L$\underline{\text{S}}$ COUVERTIE" in rectangle.

DESCRIPTION: "Fiddle" handle, up curved end with midrib; tapered shank; round, flat bowl with double drop on back at juncture with handle. "CF" script monogram on back of handle.

MEASUREMENTS: L. 34.5 cm (13⅝ in); D. bowl 9.0 cm (3³/₁₆ in); WT. 239.0 gm (7.68 oz)

LOAN: *Private Collection*

LAMOTHE

Jean-Marie Lamothe and Jean-Baptiste Lamothe were sons of master silversmith Pierre Lamothe. Their mother, Marie Couvertié Lamothe, was the daughter of Jean Couvertié and Marie Anne Brandy Couvertié, of Santo Domingo. Their uncles, Jean-Baptiste Couvertié and Louis Gabriel Couvertié, were silversmiths who worked in both Baltimore and New Orleans, following their flight from St. Marc, Santo Domingo, and Santiago de Cuba.

Jean-Marie Lamothe was born at St. Marc, on March 1, 1795. He married Marie Anne Sequin, a native of Philadelphia, daughter of Pierre Sequin and his wife, Marguerite Michau Sequin. Jean-Marie Lamothe served as a sergeant in Plauché's Battalion, Louisiana Militia, during the Battle of New Orleans in January, 1815. From 1819 to 1823, he worked with his father, Pierre Lamothe, under the name of Lamothe *et fils*. Jean-Marie Lamothe is variously known as Jean Lamothe, *Cadet* Lamothe, and Lamothe *fils*. He is last listed as a jeweler or silversmith in 1844. He died in New Orleans in 1880.

Jean-Baptiste Lamothe was born at St. Marc, Santo Domingo, on March 13, 1800. He worked with his brother from 1823 until 1844. He was married twice, to Eloise Louise Clavie and then to Elmire Pellerin. Jean-Baptiste Lamothe continued to operate a jewelry business well into the 1850s, and died in New Orleans in 1874.

The silver of the Lamothe *frères* is similar to that constructed by the elder Lamothe and the other early French artisans. It is particularly notable for its weight and heavy construction.

74. Beaker   ca. 1825-1830

MARKS (twice on bottom): "Lamothe" script letters in conforming cartouche.

DESCRIPTION: Cylindrical body; slightly tapered sides; molding on lip and base. "Emile Locoul" engraved on side. Dents removed and foot straightened by Christopher A. Hentz.

MEASUREMENTS: H. 7.9 cm (3¹/₈ in); D. Lip 6.7 cm (2⁵/₈ in); D. base 5.7 cm (2¹/₄ in); WT. 78.1 gm (2.51 oz)

PROVENANCE: Louis Raymond Emile Locoul, died in New Orleans, Louisiana, in 1879, aged 55 years. He may have been the original owner of the beaker.

Anglo-American Art Museum   77.3.1
Louisiana State University
Baton Rouge, Louisiana
Gift of the Friends of the Museum

75. Beaker ca. 1825-1830

MARK (on bottom): "Lamothe" script letters in cartouche, badly rubbed.

DESCRIPTION: Cylindrical body; applied molding on lip and base; slightly tapered sides. "Julia Benoist" engraved in script on side of body. Bad dents in sides, foot, and split in foot repaired by Christopher A. Hentz.

MEASUREMENTS: H. 7.9 cm (3¹/₁₆ in); D. lip 6.7 cm (2⁵/₈ in); D. base 5.7 cm (2¹/₄ in); WT. 80.4 gm (2.58 oz)

PROVENANCE: Marie Julie Benoist was born September 26, 1826, at Little River, Natchitoches Parish, Louisiana, and died April 15, 1870, in New Orleans. She was buried in St. Louis Cemetery #3. She was the wife of Victor Jean-Baptiste Chopin, M.D.

LOAN: *Private Collection*

76. Rice Spoon, Six Soup Spoons, and Six Forks ca. 1825-1835

MARK (on back of handles): "Lamothe" script letters in cartouches.

DESCRIPTION: "Fiddle" handles; up curved ends with mid-rib; double drop on back of bowls at juncture with handles. "JLD" engraved in script on upper back of handles.

MEASUREMENTS: RICE SPOON: L. 27.3 cm (10³/₄ in); WT. 108.6 gm (3.49 oz) SOUP SPOONS: L. each 21.0 cm (8¹/₄ in); WT. all six 397.0 gm (12.76 oz) FORKS L. each 20.6 cm (8¹/₈ in); WT. all six 419.6 gm (13.49 oz)

PROVENANCE: The DeLatte family of St. James Parish, Louisiana.

Anglo-American Art Museum 77.10.2, 77.10.3a-f,
Louisiana State University 77.10.4a-f
Baton Rouge, Louisiana
Gift of Dr. and Mrs. A. Brooks Cronan, Jr.

77.   Seal   ca. 1836

MARK (on edge): "Jⁿ Lamothe" engraved in script.

DESCRIPTION: Seal with elevation of façade of City Hall of New Orleans, enclosed within bead circle, surrounded by "PREMIERE MUNICIPALITE DE LA VILLE DE LA NOUVELLE ORLEANS" (engraved in reverse), enclosed within engraved diamond-and-bead border.

MEASUREMENTS: H. 1 cm (³/₈ in); D. 4.9 cm (1¹⁵/₁₆ in); WT. 185.9 gm (5.98 oz)

PROVENANCE: Political unrest between the French-speaking and English-speaking elements in New Orleans led the governor to sign an act dividing the city into three separate municipalities on March 8, 1836. On a motion of Mr. Armas, the Council of the First Municipality, by a resolution in French, authorized the mayor of New Orleans to commission an official seal. English translation is as follows:

> . . . In the middle of said figure of the City Hall of New Orleans and around the edge will be inscribed these words "First Municipality of the City of New Orleans" and to be paid for by the Treasury of this municipality, the cost of said official seal as well as the purchase of a press.

The official date of adoption of the new seal is unknown.

LOAN: *Mr. Louis A. J. Hernandez*
New Orleans, Louisiana

A view of the Cabildo, located on Jackson Square in New Orleans, is shown in reverse on this seal. At the time the seal was commissioned the building was used as the City Hall. It had not yet acquired its mansard roof, which was added in 1847.

The seal was replaced in 1852 by another official seal that symbolized the occasion of the reunification of the three city municipalities. The new one was designed not by a silversmith, but by an engraver and printer, John Douglas of New Orleans.

PIERRE BERTIN

There is no conclusive evidence to establish precisely who Pierre Bertin was. A Pierre Bertin turns up in 1816 in St. Martinsville, Louisiana. No Bertins have been located in the 1820 census of Louisiana. One Pierre Bertin was living in Natchitoches Parish in the 1830s, and another in New Orleans. In the 1840 census, Pierre Bertin was living in Terrebonne Parish and a Pierre Bertin died in New Orleans in the 1840s. Which of these Pierre Bertins, if any, was a silversmith is yet to be determined.

78. Ladle   ca. 1825-1835

MARK (on back of handle): "P. Bertin" script letters in engrailed rectangle.

DESCRIPTION: "Fiddle" handle; down curved end with midrib; broad bowl with flat bottom.

MEASUREMENTS: L. 38.3 cm (15¹/₈ in); D. bowl 9.85 cm (3⁷/₈ in); WT. 319.3 gm (10.27 oz)

PROVENANCE: The original owner of this piece was Blount Baker Breazeale (ca. 1801-1877) of Natchitoches Parish, Louisiana. He married in 1826 Mary Mannette Winter, daughter of William Winter of Philadelphia. Breazeale was a delegate to the Louisiana Constitutional Convention in 1844-1845. According to family tradition, this piece was commissioned in New Orleans.

Anglo-American Art Museum   79.4.5
Louisiana State University
Baton Rouge, Louisiana
Gift of Mr. and Mrs. H. Payne Breazeale, Sr.

79. Clabber Spoon   ca. 1825-1835

MARK (on back of handle): "P. Bertin" script letters in scrolled rectangle.

DESCRIPTION: 'Fiddle' handle; down curved end with midrib; long, oval bowl in continental manner with double drop on back at juncture with handle.

MEASUREMENTS: L. 30.1 cm (11⁷/₈ in); WT. 185.3 gm (5.96 oz)

PROVENANCE: Blount Baker Breazeale (see cat. no 78).

Anglo-American Art Museum   79.4.2
Louisiana State University
Baton Rouge, Louisiana
Gift of Mr. and Mrs. H. Payne Breazeale, Sr.

Blount Baker Breazeale. 1845 lithograph by Jules Lion. (The Historic New Orleans Collection 1959.13.32)

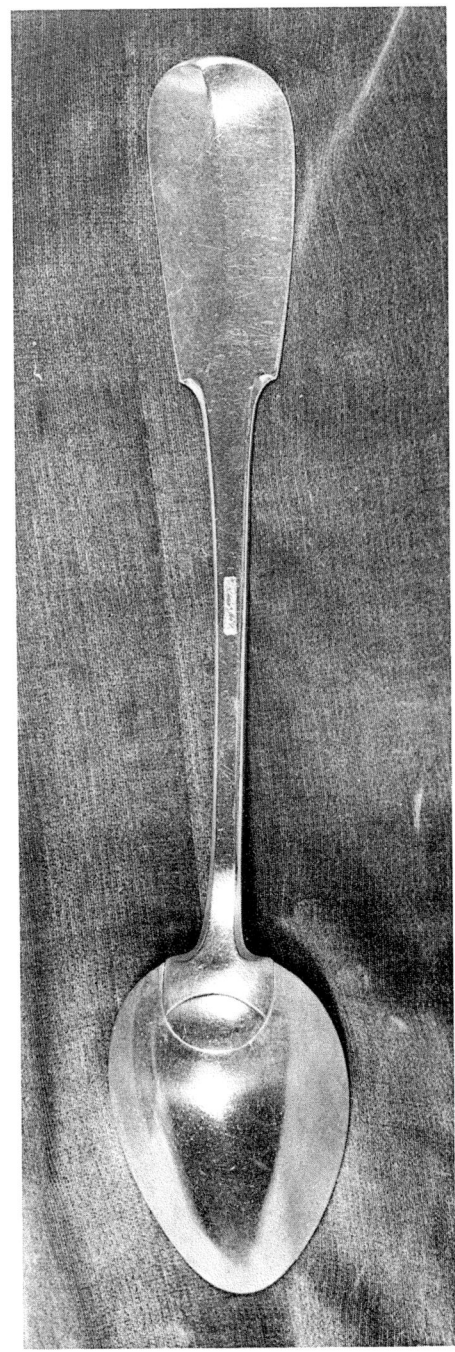

75

ANTHONY RASCH

Anthony Rasch von Tauffkirchen was born in the castle of Kleeberg, outside of Passau in Bavaria, about 1780. He was the youngest son of Count von Tauffkirchen-Kleeberg and his third wife, Gertrude Obermaier. In 1792, Rasch left Kleeberg, going to Passau, where he learned the trade of silver and goldsmithing. He married Jane Margaret Bidel of Frankfort on Main, about 1798, and then migrated to Philadelphia, between 1801 and 1803. While in the United States, Rasch dropped the "von Tauffkirchen."

In Philadelphia he was associated with Simon Chaudron, under the firm name of Chaudron and Rasch. This partnership produced examples of Neoclassical-revival and late Empire style silver. However, Chaudron and Rasch parted ways and Rasch conducted business under the name of A. Rasch and Co. He also was briefly associated with George Willig, Jr., under the partnership name of Rasch and Willig.

Rasch's first wife died in 1818, and he married Mary Fortune of Philadelphia, the following year. He spent part of 1820 in New Orleans, but returned the same year to Philadelphia to conclude his business there. With his family he permanently established himself in New Orleans by 1821. In 1836, he returned to Kleeberg to visit his relatives, also paying Paris a short visit. He returned to New Orleans by 1837, where he died in 1858.

Although Rasch produced excellent pieces of silver while in New Orleans, he was unable to duplicate in hollowware the sophistication in design or execution of the silver produced in Philadelphia.

Anthony Rasch. Undated oil painting by George Coulon. (Courtesy Mr. and Mrs. C. Layton Merritt)

80. Pitcher   ca. 1810-1820

MARKS (on inner side of foot): "A. RASCH & C°." in
rectangle, opposite; "PHILADELPHIA" in rectangle.

DESCRIPTION: High Empire style urn-shaped pitcher on
circular base; applied foliate banding at lip; applied
beading on either side of engraved zigzag band around
shoulder and on foot; applied beading at juncture of bowl
with base; cast Zeus mask applied on neck under spout;
high, arched handle with animal head at lip and terminating in leaves and rosette; cast ram's head mask on
body just below handle. "From/Mrs. Myra Clark
Gaines/To/Dr. Thomas E. Wilson/A memento of grateful esteem/for his Professional skill/and personal kind-
ness/to her Daughter./Feby. 1, 1866." script engraving
on side of body; "TEW" script monogram within
wreath.

MEASUREMENTS: H. 36.1 cm (14³/₁₆ in); D. base 11.4
cm (4¹/₂ in); W. 27.3 cm (10³/₄ in); WT. 792.4 gm
(25.48 oz)

PROVENANCE: The daughter of Mrs. Myra Clark Gaines
was a patient of Dr. Thomas E. Wilson, grandfather of
Elizabeth M. Montgomery.

The Historic New Orleans Collection   1978.103
New Orleans, Louisiana
Gift of Miss Elizabeth M. Montgomery

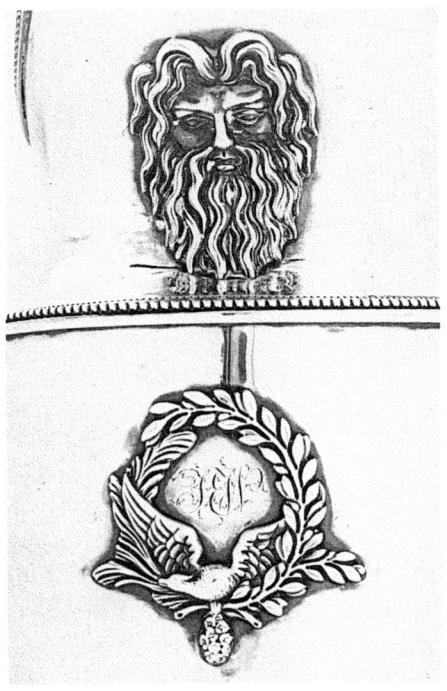

Myra Clark Gaines was the daughter of Daniel Clark and Marie Julie (Zulime) Carriere De-
Grange. Separated from her mother and abandoned
by her father, she was raised in a foster home in
Philadelphia. When she discovered her true parent-
age, she launched an historic legal battle lasting
fifty years to claim her father's immense estate
which included 3,465 acres of valuable land within
the city of New Orleans. Her attorneys' fees ran to
$600,000 as several prominent New Orleans law-
yers brought the case before the United States
Supreme Court eleven times. After her death her
heirs were awarded $500,000, only a fraction of the
wealth she had sought to recover.

The pitcher was made by Anthony Rasch in
Philadelphia during the time Myra Clark was living
there with her foster parents. It may have been
brought with her to New Orleans, and then, many
years after it was made, engraved and presented to
Dr. Wilson.

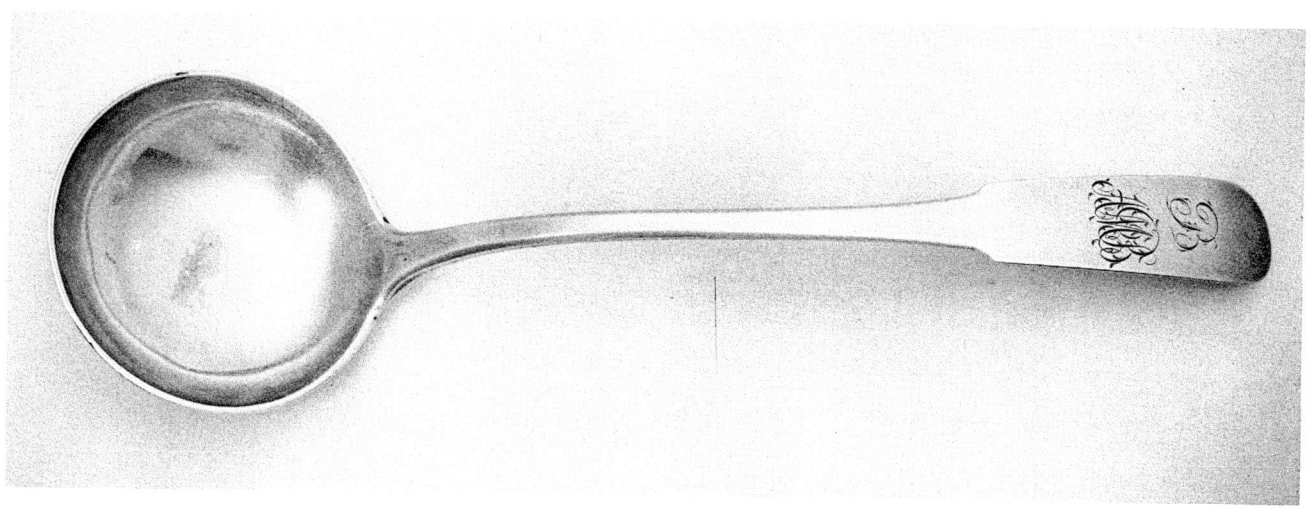

81. Ladle   ca. 1820-1850

MARKS (on back of handle): "A. RASCH." in rectangle, to left of "N. ORLEAИS" in rectangle.

DESCRIPTION: "Fiddle" handle; down curved end with short midrib; tapered to circular, flat bowl with single drop on back at juncture with handle. "B" engraved in script, above; "AMB" engraved in script on upper face of handle.

MEASUREMENTS: L. 35.6 cm (14 in.); D. bowl 9.7 cm (3³/₁₆ in); WT. 215.2 gm (6.92 oz)

The Historic New Orleans Collection   1978.175.70
New Orleans, Louisiana

82. Gravy or Stew Spoon   ca. 1820-1840

MARKS (on back of handle): "A. RASCH" in rectangle, to left of; "N. ORLEAИS" in rectangle.

DESCRIPTION: "Shell" pattern; heavy construction; single drop on back of ovoid bowl at juncture with handle; no shoulders. "CGO" engraved in script on back of handle.

MEASUREMENTS: L. 30.8 cm (12⁷/₈ in); WT. 153.5 gm (4.94 oz)

PROVENANCE: This spoon was part of the table silver of Mr. James A. Stouse's great-grandparents, Charles Gustave Oemichen and Caroline Vignaud Oemichen. It was given to Mr. Stouse by his uncle, Mr. Albert Stouse, son of Joseph Albert Stouse and Amalia Oemichen Stouse.

The Historic New Orleans Collection   1977.308.2
New Orleans, Louisiana
Gift of Mr. James A. Stouse

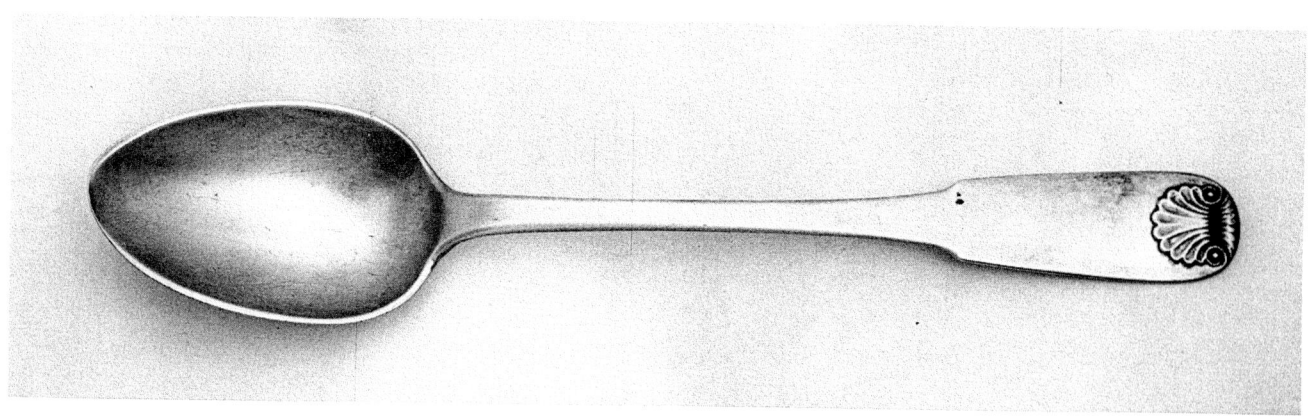

83. Dessert Spoon, Tablespoon, Dinner Fork, Dessert Fork, and Three Teaspoons   ca. 1820-1830

MARKS (on back of handle of right teaspoon): "F & G" in rectangle; (on back of handle of all other pieces): "A. RASCH" in rectangle, left; "N. ORLEANS" in rectangle.

DESCRIPTION: "Shell and thread" pattern; heavily constructed; single drop on back of bowls at juncture with handles; modified sugar-loaf shoulders. "OLDHAM" engraved in script on back of handles; unidentified crest engraved on upper face of handle. McCall crest, a boot couped at the calf per proper and spurred, engraved on back of handles (of teaspoons only).

MEASUREMENTS: DESSERT SPOON: L. 19.1 cm (7½ in); WT. 70.9 gm (2.27 oz) TABLESPOON: L. 22.6 cm (8¹⁵/₁₆ in); WT. 108.8 gm (3.50 oz) DINNER FORK: L. 21.5 cm (8½ in); WT. 105.7 gm (3.40 oz) DESSERT FORK: 18.6 gm (7³/₈ in); WT. 83.2 gm (2.67 oz) TEASPOONS: LEFT: L.15.4 cm (6¹/₁₆ in): WT. 30.3 gm (.97 oz); CENTER: L.15.2 cm (6 in); WT. 30.1 gm (.97 oz); RIGHT: L. 15.6 cm (6¹/₈ in); WT. 30.1 gm (.97 oz)

LOAN: *Mr. Harry McCall, Jr.*
New Orleans, Louisiana
and
Private Collection

The Fletcher and Gardiner "shell and thread" pattern on the far right spoon may have been the prototype for the Rasch "shell and thread" pattern on the other two spoons. Fletcher and Gardiner was an influential silversmithing firm in Philadelphia from about 1815 to 1830—a time when Rasch was working there and then also in New Orleans. Anthony Rasch—as a former Philadelphia resident relocated in New Orleans—could have brought these styles to the city by importing such flatware and by casting his own copies of the original Fletcher and Gardiner pieces. Together, the "OLDHAM" flatware and the teaspoons from the McCall family show that there were at least five types of utensils available from Rasch in this pattern. All were heavily constructed by Rasch in the manner prevalent among his French contemporaries in New Orleans.

84. Pair of Pitchers   ca. 1830-1840

MARKS (on bottom): "A. RASCH" in rectangle, struck
     twice, one inverted.

DESCRIPTION: Late Empire style inverted pear-shaped
     bodies; applied, double banding of gadrooning and
     anthemion-in-open-heart at lip, shoulder, stem, and
     as vertical foot on each; leaf-capped "S"-scroll handles
     with spurs.

MEASUREMENTS: H. each 29.7 cm (11^{11}/$_{16}$ in); D. bowl
     each 16.5 cm (6^1/$_2$ in); D. base each 11.4 cm (4^1/$_2$ in);
     WTS. 1170.5 gm (37.63 oz); 1205.3 gm (38.74 oz)

PROVENANCE: Pandelli family of New Orleans.

LOAN: *Private Collection*

85. Pitcher   ca. 1856

MARK (on underside of base): "A. RASCH" in rectangle.

DESCRIPTION: Pear-shaped body on dome-shaped pedestal base; cast ring border of palmettes at juncture of bowl with base; repoussé scrolling foliage and flowers covering most of body and base and forming reserve at front opposite handle; chased vine border encircling base just above foot; curved handle with spurs. "This cup is a gift sent to the man who in his generosity has done a thousand favors." engraved in Hebrew within reserve on body. (Translated by the Reverend Charles Wood, Chaplain, Episcopal Student Center, Louisiana State University, Baton Rouge.) "Presented/to Br. M. Bettman, G.N.A./by the Brothers of Gan Eden Lodge, Nº 24. I.O.B.B./New Orleans/as a token of Respect, Brotherly Love and Harmony./January 22, 1856. (5616)" script engraving also within reserve; "PRESENTED/ TO HIS/FIRST GRANDSON/Jeoffrey Bettman/

FROM HIS GRANDPA/CINCINNATI JUNE 26th 1888" engraved below spout.

MEASUREMENTS: H. 27.9 cm (11 in); D. base 12.7 cm (5 in); W. 20.9 cm (8¹/₄ in); WT. 819.4 gm (26.34 oz)

PROVENANCE: The Bettman family is prominent in Cincinnati. Apparently M. Bettman never lived in New Orleans and was presented with this pitcher for favors he had done for the members of Gan Eden Lodge of the International Order of B'nai B'rith. The pitcher was given to his grandson and passed out of the family at some time in the twentieth century.

Anglo-American Art Museum 78.16
Louisiana State University
Baton Rouge, Louisiana
Gift of the Friends of the Museum

HENRY HARLAND

Henry Harland was born in 1789 at Norwich, Connecticut, the son of Thomas Harland, watch and clockmaker, and his wife, Hannah Clark Harland. Harland was probably trained in his father's establishment and came to New Orleans after the Battle of New Orleans in January of 1815.

During 1815, Harland announced in New Orleans newspapers that Hemsted and Wallach, watchmakers of New York, would be at his store on Conti Street, opposite the American Coffeehouse. He displayed and sold their merchandise, and also advertised the repair of their watches. In 1819, Harland moved his establishment from Conti to 25 Chartres Street, between Bienville and Customhouse. He moved back to Conti Street, and then moved again, to 18 Chartres, in 1823.

After January, 1830, Harland formed a partnership with H. Bliss in New Orleans, under the name of Harland & Bliss. Bliss died in New Orleans in September of 1830. By December, 1830, Harland had formed another partnership, this time with Daniel Blair, formerly of St. Louis, Missouri. The partnership of Harland & Blair lasted until 1834, although Harland is last listed in the New Orleans directories in 1832.

Harland seems to have commuted between Norwich, Connecticut, and New Orleans. He married Abigail Leffingwell Hyde, daughter of John and Sarah Russell Leffingwell Hyde, in Norwich in 1822. Abigail was related on her father's side to James Nevins Hyde and on her mother's to Hyde's partner, Charles Whiting Goodrich. Also, all of Henry Harland's children were born in Norwich, from 1823 to 1837. Examples of Harland's work survive in both the northeast and New Orleans. He appears to have used the same mark in both Norwich and New Orleans, and even continued to use his father's old strike. Henry Harland died in Norwich, Connecticut, in 1841.

86. Urn   ca. 1831

MARKS (on bottom of bowl): "HARLAND" in banner, with star in circle and "D" in rectangle at each end; lion facing right in profile, male facing right, and "S" in rounded rectangles above scroll.

DESCRIPTION: Shallow, bowl-shaped body with lip curved in, to applied high, flared neck; cast beaded band applied at juncture of body and neck, band of cast grapes and grapevine applied on matted ground at neck, and applied cast lip in form of convex egg-and-dart molding below vertical edge; two cast, scrolled, acanthus bail handles on body, with large leaf junctures; body on applied, cast, beaded band; applied vertical beaded edge to foot, in form of stamped, scrolled, acanthus decoration on matted ground. "To H M Dobbs President of the New-Orleans Mechanic Society" engraved on one side of bowl over device of craftman's insignia; "Presented by the members in testimony of respect/for 25 years faithful services/ Jany 22d 1831" engraved on other side.

MEASUREMENTS: H. 25.2 cm (9^{15}/$_{16}$ in); D. lip 19.2 cm (7^9/$_{16}$ in); D. base 11.6 cm (4^9/$_{16}$ in); W. 21.9 cm (8^5/$_8$ in); WT. 1241.0 gm (39.90 oz)

PROVENANCE: Henry M. Dobbs, Sr., was born ca. 1765, probably in New York City. He was a watchmaker and operated the watchmaking business of John J. Staples, Jr., New York, 1793-1794; thereafter operating his own business until his first retirement in 1802, when succeeded by Bannister and Upjohn. However, by November of 1803, Dobbs had returned to his old stand where he continued to operate until a disastrous fire in December of 1804. He does not appear in the 1805 census of New Orleans, but he must have moved there sometime in 1805. In 1806, with several others, Dobbs founded the New Orleans Mechanic Society, composed of mechanics, manufacturers, and artists associated "To Relieve the wants, comfort the sufferings and promote the happiness of our fellow creatures." Henry M. Dobbs was the first president of the organization from its founding in 1806 until 1831. He died in 1836. Henry Harland, the maker of this urn, was the tenth member of the Society.

LOAN: *Yale University Art Gallery 1936.160*
New Haven, Connecticut
Mabel Brady Garvan Collection

83

HARLAND & BLAIR

Harland & Blair was a partnership between Henry Harland and Daniel Blair. It appears to have been formed immediately following the dissolution of the partnership of Harland & Bliss, occasioned by the death of Bliss in September, 1830. By December of that same year, the new firm was already advertising its operation.

Daniel Blair, formerly of St. Louis, Missouri, had been in partnership with John Daggett in St. Louis from 1821. The partnership was dissolved several years before 1830. After moving to New Orleans, Daniel Blair returned briefly to St. Louis to marry Lucinda Sparks, sister of John Daggett's wife. He later purchased a slave from Daggett, the sale being recorded in the New Orleans Conveyance Office.

The partnership of Harland & Blair was relatively short-lived. By 1834 Daniel Blair was in partnership with William Hazard; he then became a partner in Whittemore & Blair, and later Blair & Lawes, after 1840.

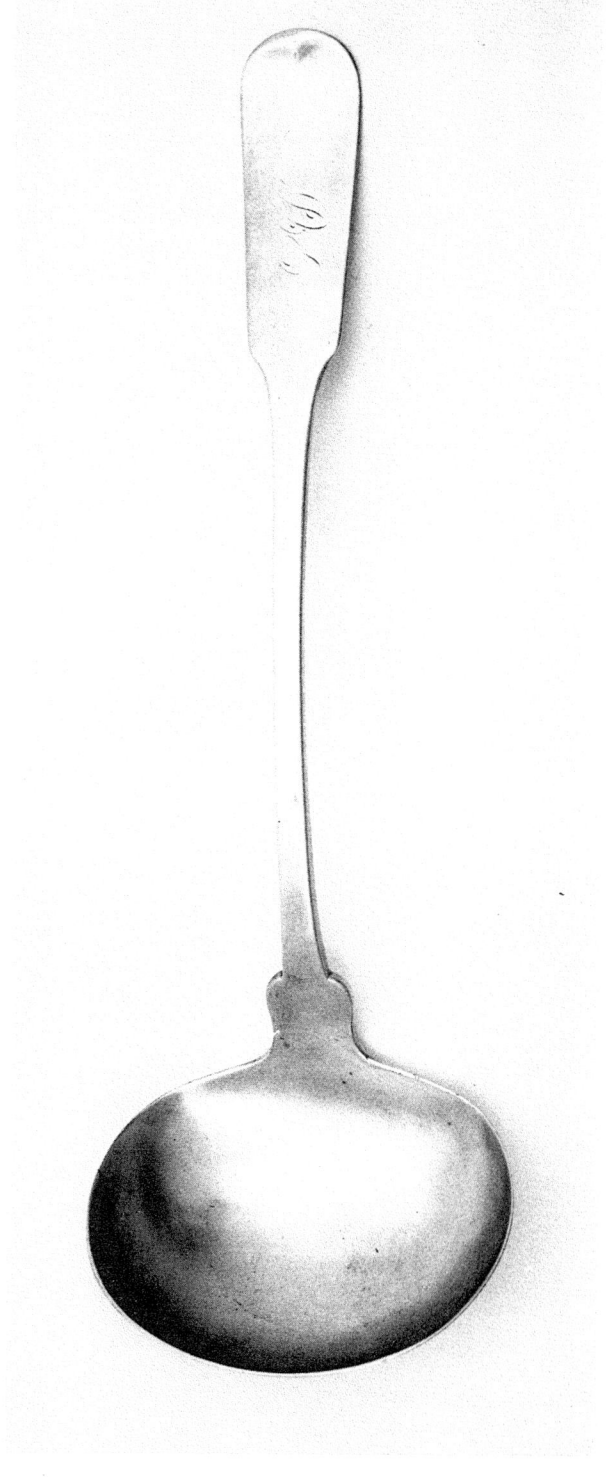

87. Ladle   ca. 1830-1834

MARK (on back of handle): "HARLAND & BLAIR" in rectangle.

DESCRIPTION: "Fiddle" handle, up curved tipped end, tapered slightly to round shoulders; oval bowl with single drop on back at juncture with handle. "PAD" engraved in script on upper face of handle.

MEASUREMENTS: L. 34.5 cm (13⅝ in); D. bowl 10.5 cm (4⅛ in); WT. 211.3 gm (6.79 oz)

PROVENANCE: This ladle was given to Mr. James A. Stouse by his mother, Mrs. Coralie Ducros Stouse. It and two small salt spoons (not illustrated) are all that is left of the table service from its original owners, Pierre Adolphe Ducros and his wife, Adelaide Adele de La Ronde.

The Historic New Orleans Collection   1977.308.1
New Orleans, Louisiana
Gift of Mr. James A. Stouse

84

BROWER

The partnership of Samuel and Baldwin Brower, known as S. & B. Brower, 17 Camp Street, existed in New Orleans after September, 1833, as a southern branch of S. & B. Brower of Albany, New York. It was familiar in New Orleans as a furnishing warehouse and fancy hardware store, selling lamps, silver, and plated wares.

In early 1834, a presentation pitcher was commissioned from Messrs. Brower as a testimonial for services rendered by the Mississippi Fire Company No. 2, during a fire on board the Steamboat *Missourian*. Its whereabouts is presently unknown.

Following the dissolution of the partnership, Baldwin Brower formed B. Brower & Co. with his brother, George C. Brower, pursuant to Articles of Co-Partnership made in Northhampton, Massachusetts, in 1842. The new firm continued to operate at 17 Camp Street as a "House Furnishing Store."

Baldwin Brower died in 1845, at Palermo, Italy, age thirty-four years. His interest in the firm was continued by his wife, Elizabeth Barker Brower, until 1849. In 1849 the partnership was reformed, without change of name, by George C. Brower and William T. Vanzandt, second husband of Elizabeth Barker Brower. B. Brower & Co. was dissolved by *cessio bonorum* in 1855. George C. Brower died at Selma, Alabama, in 1864.

The earlier firm of S. & B. Brower, or just Brower, was a silver manufacturer. The company produced both flatware and hollowware, but is distinguished by the latter in the Classical revival or Empire style. The later firm, B. Brower & Co., was primarily an importer.

88. Pair of Pitchers   ca. 1833-1835

MARKS (on bottom of bowls): "BROWER" in arc, above; "17 CAMP ST." in rectangle, above; "NEW ORLEANS" in arc.

DESCRIPTION: Late Classical-revival or Empire style round bodies on conforming pedestal bases; applied, bold bandings of anthemia-in-open-hearts at lip, shoulder, base, stem, and as vertical foot of each; high, leaf-capped, reeded, curved handles.

MEASUREMENTS: LEFT: H. 33.9 cm (13½ in); D. base 12.5 cm (4¹⁵/₁₆ in); W. 23.5 cm (9¼ in); WT. 1057.6 gm (34.00 oz.) RIGHT: H. 33.9 cm (13½ in); D. base 12.7 cm (5 in); W. 23.5 cm (9¼ in); WT. 1076.2 gm (34.60 oz)

LOAN: *Private Collection*

BLISS & WHITTEMORE

Bliss & Whittemore was a partnership between John Bliss and Edwin Whittemore from 1833 to 1835.

In 1830, John Bliss of New Orleans married Miss Abby Williams in Canaan, New York. Bliss worked as a watchmaker on Chartres Street until forming the partnership with Whittemore. There is no record of Bliss in New Orleans after 1835.

Edwin Whittemore, a native of Worcester, Massachusetts, was involved in several silversmithing partnerships: Coit & Whittemore, Natchez, Mississippi, active 1830-1833; Bliss & Whittemore; Whittemore & Blair, New Orleans, active 1838-1840; and Whittemore & [Nelson A.] Young, New Orleans, active 1840-1841. Whittemore died in New Orleans in 1867, in his sixty-ninth year.

The northeastern backgrounds of Bliss and Whittemore are apparent in the silver produced by the firm. The partnership appears to have been uninfluenced by the popular French styles prevalent in New Orleans.

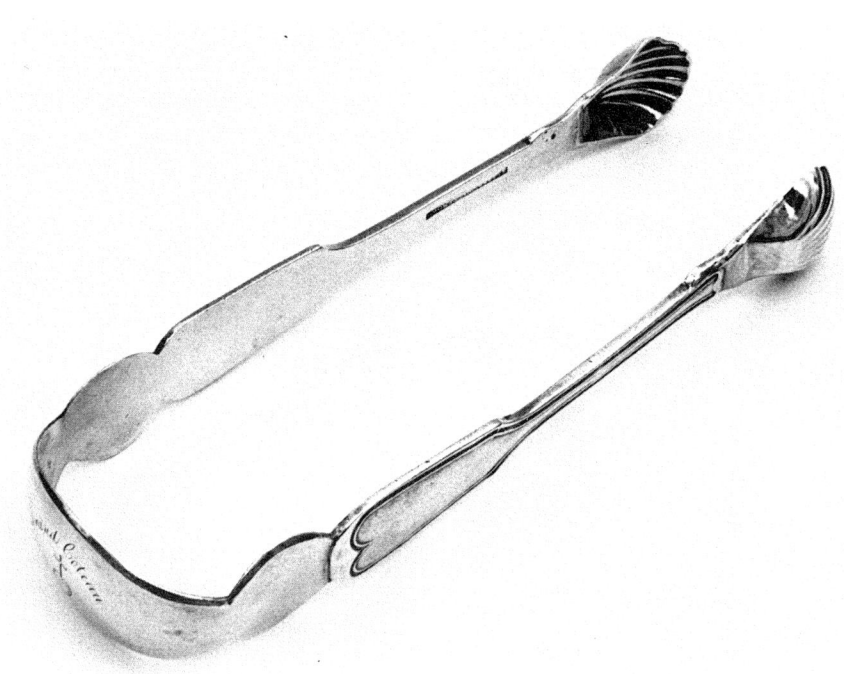

89. Tongs   ca. 1833-1835

MARK (on inside of arm): "BLISS & WHITTEMORE" in rectangle.

DESCRIPTION: "Fiddle thread" handle terminating in shell grips. "Grand Coteau" engraved in arc on upper face of handle at curve, above; engraved cross, above; engraved heart.

MEASUREMENTS: L. 16.2 cm (6³/₈ in); W. 5.8 cm (2⁵/₁₆ in); WT. 85.5 gm (2.75 oz)

PROVENANCE: These tongs bear the crest of the Order of the Sacred Heart, an order of nuns who have run the Convent School of the Sacred Heart at Grand Coteau near Lafayette, Louisiana, since the 1830s. These tongs were the property of the convent until they were sold to the present owners.

LOAN: *The Holden Family Collection Baton Rouge, Louisiana*

WHITTEMORE & BLAIR

Whittemore & Blair, or frequently Whittemore, Blair & Co., was a partnership between Edwin Whittemore and Daniel Blair, from 1838-1840. Whittemore, originally from Worcester, Massachusetts, had been a member of a number of previous partnerships in the New Orleans area. He remained in New Orleans until his death in 1867.

Daniel Blair was also involved in several other silversmithing partnerships: Daggett & Blair, St. Louis, Missouri, active 1821-before 1830;

Harland & Blair, New Orleans, active 1830-1834; Hazard & Blair, New Orleans, active 1834; and Blair & Lawes, New Orleans, active after 1840. No known silver pieces survive from the last two alliances.

Apparently the firm of Whittemore & Blair was beset by financial difficulties from the first day its doors opened to the public. The business was dissolved in 1840, leaving a large gathering of creditors.

90. Coffee and Tea Service   ca. 1837-1841

MARKS (on bottom of each piece): "WHITTEMORE & BLAIR" in rectangle, struck twice; pseudo-hallmarks, a male bust and an eagle, each in ovals.

DESCRIPTION: Round, widely fluted, melon-shaped bodies; small gadrooned and beaded borders; applied collar bandings of stylized drops and foliage; high, fluted, domed lids with knob-like finials; molded pedestal bases; swan-neck spout and insulated, silver, scroll handle on coffee and tea pots; two cast bail handles on body of sugar bowl. Dents knocked out of bowls of all pieces. Each piece's stepped base had been compressed somewhat and had to be raised. The handles of both pots have been straightened and two silver handle pins have been replaced. The coffee pot has had a split rib seam and three splits in the stepped base brazed. The lid of the sugar bowl is a reconstruction made by Louisiana State University metalsmithing students, Ellis Joubert and Thomas Lorio, under the supervision of Christopher A. Hentz, who executed the other repairs.

MEASUREMENTS: COFFEE POT: H. 27.7 cm (10⅞ in); D. base 11.7 cm (4⅝ in); W. 29.2 cm (11½ in); WT. 981.1 gm (31.54 oz) TEA POT: H. 26.0 cm (10¼ in); D. base 10.8 cm (4½ in); W. 27.7 cm (10⅞ in); WT. 896.4 gm (28.82 oz); SUGAR BOWL: H. without lid 17.2 cm (6¾ in); D. base 10.5 cm (4⅛ in); W. 20.3 cm (8 in); WT. without lid 633.8 gm (20.38 oz)

PROVENANCE: Sotheby Parke Bernet, Inc., New York; Sale 4211, Item 54; January 31, 1979.

Anglo-American Art Museum   79.31.1-3
Louisiana State University
Baton Rouge, Louisiana

No single firm in New Orleans had exclusive rights to the retailing of another company's wares. A similar service in the Bayou Bend Collection (not illustrated), consisting of a tea pot, sugar bowl, and a waste, bears the same pseudo-hallmarks; but it was retailed in New Orleans through Hyde & Goodrich. The pseudo-hallmarks of both services have been attributed to Gale, Wood & Hughes of New York.

M. SCOOLER

Maurice Scooler was born in Wurzburg, Bavaria, in 1827. He arrived in New Orleans about 1842, and was employed by a jeweler in the Third District. Around 1848 he opened his own establishment and continued in business until his death in 1900. He married Mary Ann Levy, niece of Commodore Uriah Levy.

Scooler was primarily an importer of finished goods. Following the Civil War, his firm manufactured "krewe favors" for various carnival organizations' Mardi Gras balls.

M. Scooler's store clock, corner of Canal and Royal Streets. Detail of 1894 photograph. (Courtesy The Historic New Orleans Collection 1974.25.8.232)

"M. Scooler's Establishment," 615-617 Canal Street. Ca. 1890-1900 photograph. (Courtesy Nat Halpern, Jr.)

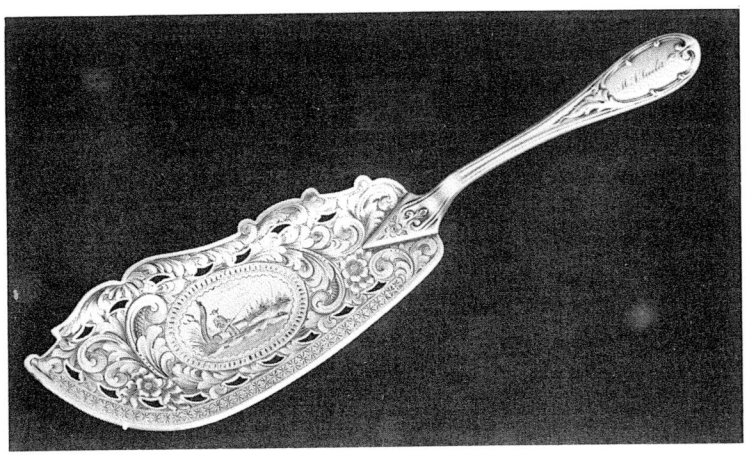

91. Fish Knife ca. 1848-1849

MARKS (on back of handle): "M. SCOOLER" in rectangle; (on back of blade): eagle in circle, above; "V" in lozenge, above; male head in circle.

DESCRIPTION: "Tuscan" pattern variation handle; elaborate, leafy, scroll engraving, flower heads, and pierced drains surrounding picturesque engraved oval vignette of fisherman; engraved pinwheel border along blade edge. "M. A. Scooler" engraved in script on upper face of handle.

MEASUREMENTS: L. 30.9 cm (12³/₁₆ in); W. 7.1 cm (2⁹/₁₆ in); WT. 139.7 gm (4.49 oz)

PROVENANCE: Mary Ann Levy, niece of Commodore Urian Levy, was the wife of Maurice Scooler. She died in 1919.

LOAN: *Private Collection*

This piece is attributed to George C. Vaughn, Buffalo, and was retailed through Scooler in New Orleans. The fishing scene is a charming variation from the usual fish profile found on the knives retailed by Hyde and Goodrich (cat. nos. 20 and 21).

92. Buckle ca. 1890

MARK (on back): "M. SCOOLER N.O." incised.

DESCRIPTION: Lady's rectangular belt buckle; bright-cut engraving of rosettes and foliage.

MEASUREMENTS: H. 8.0 cm (3¹/₈ in); W. 5.4 cm (2¹/₈ in); WT. 34.4 gm (1.11 oz)

Anglo-American Art Museum 79.8.1
Louisiana State University
Baton Rouge, Louisiana
Gift of the Friends of the Museum

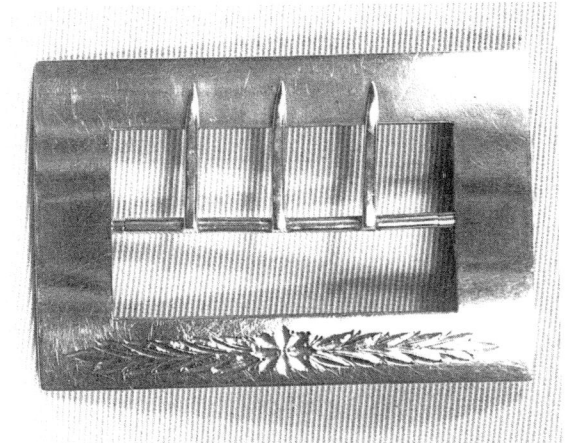

93. Buckle ca. 1891

MARK (on back): "M. SCOOLER N.O." incised.

DESCRIPTION: Lady's rectangular belt buckle with serpentine edge; wrigglework engraving around edge. "Mrs. J. H. DeGrange/1891" engraved in script on back.

MEASUREMENTS: H. 8.5 cm (3³/₈ in); W. 5.1 cm (2 in); WT. 36.1 gm (1.16 oz)

PROVENANCE: Mrs. Joseph H. DeGrange (neé Ellen McMillan) died March 5, 1910. Her husband was a New Orleans railway executive.

LOAN: *Mr. and Mrs. James H. Adams, Jr.*
New Orleans, Louisiana

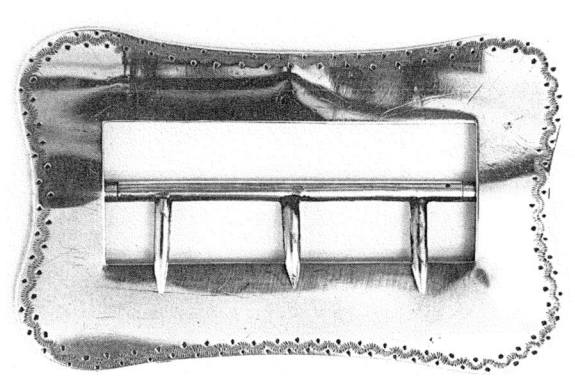

Each year a number of independent organizations in New Orleans, calling themselves *krewes*, celebrate what is known here as *carnival*. The merriment continues from Twelfth Night, January 6, through Shrove Tuesday, Mardi Gras day. Each krewe holds a lavish ball, when costumed and masked members invite, or "call out," ladies for the dances, after which the maskers present "favors," or small presents, to their partners.

It is believed that this practice originated at the twenty-fifth anniversary ball of the Mistick Krewe of Comus, 1882, and was adopted by other krewes. Handsome pins were often commissioned through New Orleans's silver firms and were designed to reflect the theme of the parade or tableau ball.

The Rex pin (cat. no. 94) dates from the Mardi Gras celebration of Tuesday, February 14, 1888. The parade, followed by a reception at the Royal Opera House, had for its theme "The Realm of Flowers." The Rex invitation opened to display a garden paradise; its silhouette was inspired by the butterfly on the pin.

Maurice Scooler used crossed Persian scimitars flanking the organization's monogram when he made the pin for the Krewe of Proteus (cat. no. 95). The pageant of "Shah Nameh, the Epic of the Kings," celebrated on February 5, 1894, was beautifully illustrated on a colorful fan-shaped invitation.

The "captain" of Rex, 1896, coordinated every detail of that year's celebration, "Heavenly Bodies". Scooler's "call-out" favor (cat. no. 96) was a silver replica of the group's invitation. The shiny silver highlights on the card produced even greater radiance when the details were executed in bright-cut engraving on the pin.

94. Carnival Pin   1888

MARK (on back): "M. SCOOLER N.O." incised.

DESCRIPTION: Pierced engraved crown above banner; large butterfly with engraved wings, antennae, and body attached at band of crown. "REX" engraved across crown.

MEASUREMENTS: H. 3.2 cm (1¼ in); W. 3.8 cm (1½ in); WT. 6.5 gm (.21 oz)

Anglo-American Art Museum   78.12
Louisiana State University
Baton Rouge, Louisiana
Gift of the Friends of the Museum

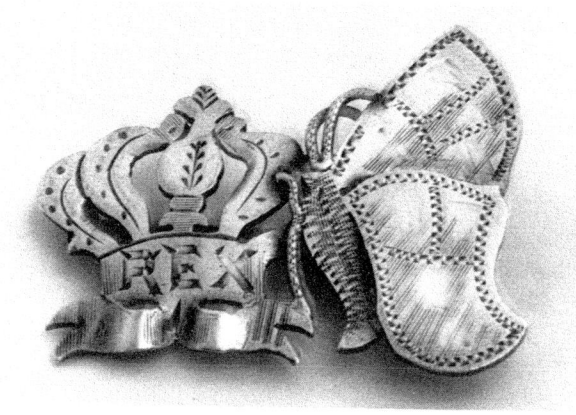

Rex invitation. 1888 color lithograph. (The Historic New Orleans Collection 1960.14.80)

95. Carnival Pin 1894

MARK (on back): "M. SCOOLER N.O." incised.

DESCRIPTION: Silver-gilt crowned cipher "KOP" flanked by scimitars crossed at handles and by foliate motifs; "18" engraved on left blade, "94" engraved on right blade.

MEASUREMENTS: L. 4.0 cm (1⁹/₁₆ in); W. 3.2 cm (1¹/₄ in); WT. 6.8 gm (.22 oz)

The Historic New Orleans Collection   1979.254.78
New Orleans, Louisiana

Krewe of Proteus invitation. 1894 color lithograph. (The Historic New Orleans Collection 1960.14.57)

96. Carnival Pin 1896

MARK (on back): "M. SCOOLER N.O." incised.

DESCRIPTION: Crowned, cloud-shrouded planet showing phases of moon in seriatum. "REX" engraved in clouds; "1896" engraved across band of crown.

MEASUREMENTS: H. 4.8 cm (1⁷/₈ in); W. 4.0 cm (1⁹/₁₆ in); WT. 7.9 gm (.25 oz)

The Historic New Orleans Collection   1979.254.83
New Orleans, Louisiana

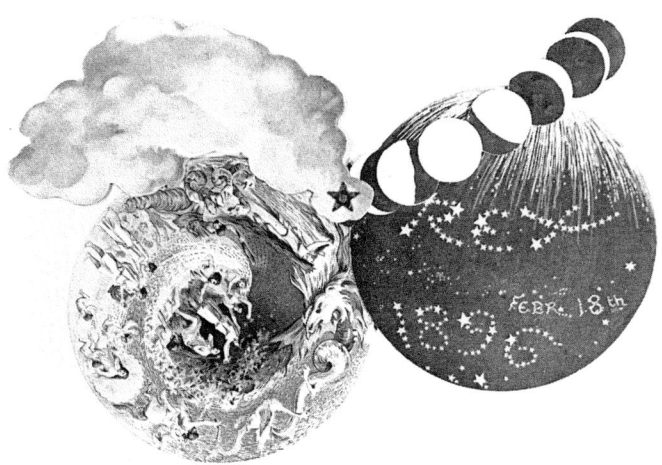

Rex invitation. 1896 color lithograph. (The Historic New Orleans Collection 1974.25.19.657)

H. E. BALDWIN & CO.

Horace E. Baldwin was a partner in Taylor, Baldwin & Company of Newark, New Jersey. He opened a New Orleans branch of the jewelry and silver manufacturing firm in 1842. It appears to have been discontinued after 1853.

Most of the silver hollowware and flatware sold by H.E. Baldwin & Co. in New Orleans was probably made in the New Jersey and New York area.

97. Beaker   ca. 1842-1851

MARKS (on bottom): "H. E. BALDWIN & CO." in arc, above; star, above; "NEW ORLEANS" in rectangle, above; "WF" in rectangle; beaver in oval, at either end of arc.

DESCRIPTION: Serpentine, hexagonal body with straight, tapering sides; applied molding at lip. "S. Baitor Hinckley Jr./The Future Midshipman/From/Lieut Wm. B. Cushing/Jan/19th 1864" engraved in script on side.

MEASUREMENTS: H. 9.0 cm (3⁹/₁₆ in); D. lip 7.9 cm (3¹/₈ in); D. base 6.5 cm (2⁹/₁₆ in); WT. 135.7 gm (4.36 oz)

LOAN: *The Museum of Fine Arts*
The Bayou Bend Collection
Houston, Texas
Gift of Wunsch Americana Foundation

The incised "WF" has been attributed to William Forbes, who worked in New York from 1827 or 1828 until 1850.

98. Cup ca. 1842-1853

MARKS (on bottom of bowl): "H. E. BALDWIN & Co" in arc, above; "NEW ORLEANS" in rectangle, above; "MANUFACTURERS" in complementary arc.

DESCRIPTION: Octagonal, slightly bulbous body on applied octagonal foot with spool-shaped shaft; molded lip; simple curved handle with thumbpiece. "A Mother's Gift" engraved in script on front. Poor repairs made to the handle at the juncture of the bowl prior to acquisition by the present owner. Foot straightened by Christopher A. Hentz.

MEASUREMENTS: H. 14.6 cm (5³/₄ in); D. lip 8.5 cm (3⁷/₈ in); D. base 7.5 cm (2¹⁵/₁₆ in); W. 12.4 (4⁷/₈ in); WT. 170.3 gm (5.48 oz)

Anglo-American Art Museum 79.42
Louisiana State University
Baton Rouge, Louisiana
Gift of the Friends of the Museum

99. Pitcher ca. 1842-1853

MARKS (on bottom): "H. E. BALDWIN & Co" in arc, above; "NEW ORLEANS" in rectangle above; "MANUFACTURERS" in complementary arc; "J.B." in rectangle.

DESCRIPTION: Vase-shaped body; applied borders of open hearts and foliate motif against striated ground at lip, collar, and reversed on vertical foot; engraved Rococo-revival foliage and flower on body, forming cartouche on each side; three sailboats engraved in one reserve; scroll handle with spurs. "ACF" script monogram on side.

MEASUREMENTS: H. 30.9 cm (12¹/₄ in); D. base 11.4 cm (4¹/₂ in); W. 20.3 cm (8 in); WT. 905.3 (29.11 oz)

PROVENANCE: Charles Mulholland Flower Family, Evergreen Plantation, Alexandria, Louisiana.

LOAN: *Mrs. Carol Flower Layton*
Monroe, Louisiana

JAMES A. YOUNG

James A. Young is listed in the 1842 New Orleans city directories as a watchmaker, working at 94 St. Charles. It is entirely possible that he was an itinerant watchmaker who only briefly lived in New Orleans.

100. Buckle   ca. 1842-1843

MARK (on reverse): "J. YOUNG N.O." incised.

DESCRIPTION: Gentleman's gold-faced, coin silver buckle; curved rectangular frame surrounding three pierced, interlaced script initials "GLS"; decorated with engraved lines; engraved foliate designs at each corner of frame.

MEASUREMENTS: H. 3.2 cm (1¼ in); W. 5.1 cm (2 in); WT. 20.3 gm (.65 oz)

Anglo-American Art Museum   79.3.2
Louisiana State University
Baton Rouge, Louisiana
Gift of the Friends of the Museum

C. REDON

Claudius Redon was born in France in 1788. He was working in New York around 1828. In 1830, Redon advertised that he was opening his establishment at 103 Chartres Street, between Conti and St. Louis Streets, in New Orleans.

By 1845, he had moved to the corner of St. Charles and Common Streets, and by 1849 had moved again, to the corner of Customhouse and Chartres Streets.

At this last location he spent over $3,000, fitting out the store and residence leased from Cordevidle. The landlord refused to make certain repairs to the building, which became uninhabitable. By 1851, Redon made plans to move, but Cordevidle, in an effort to enforce his lessor's lien, seized the contents of Redon's store. The value of the merchandise, a general assortment of jewelry and silver, was $10,791.66. In the litigation which followed, Redon was victorious, but he appears not to have resumed his business.

Claudius Redon died in New Orleans in 1857.

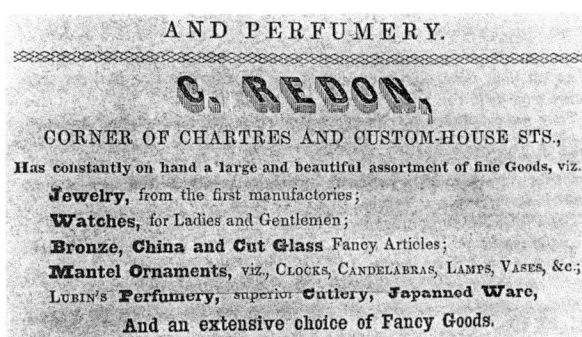

C. Redon advertisement. *Cohen's New Orleans and Lafayette Directory.* New Orleans: Printed at the office of the Daily Delta, 1849. (The Historic New Orleans Collection)

101. Pitcher ca. 1843

MARK (on bottom): "C. REDON" in rectangle.

DESCRIPTION: Classical vase body with concave flutes; applied, beaded band at lip; applied, bold, egg-and-dart band at shoulder; fluted collar at juncture of spool shaft with body; round, domed, fluted base with applied, vertical foot banding of water leaves against a striated ground; double "C"-scroll handle with thumbpiece. "Awarded/to the/Washington Guards/at a third trial of skills in Target Practice with the/Harrison Guards./April 1843./New Orleans./Distance 60 yards./25 men each. 75 shots./W. G. 61 in 75./H. G. 60 in 75." engraved on body.

MEASUREMENTS: H. 34.0 cm (13³⁄₈ in); D. base 13.0 cm (5³⁄₁₆ in); W. 27.0 cm (10⁵⁄₈ in); WT. 1047.6 gm (33.68 oz)

PROVENANCE: Colonel James B. Walton (see cat. no. 41).

LOAN: *Mr. James B. Norris*
Pass Christian, Mississippi

French presentation pitcher. (Courtesy Private Collection, photograph by Jean Jeffers)

The Washington Guard, now known as the Washington Artillery, is the oldest military organization in the state of Louisiana. This pitcher was given to the Washington Guards by the Harrison Guard at a third trial of skills. The second trial of skill in target practice was also won by the Washington Guards, and the prize awarded at that match was a French pitcher.

E. A. TYLER

Edward A. Tyler was born in Boston in 1815. He was apprenticed to a watchmaking and jewelry business when he was fourteen years old. He worked in Belfast, Maine, for four years starting in 1834.

In 1838, Tyler moved to New Orleans and, with a friend, established the partnership of Tyler & Jacks. The partnership was dissolved when Jacks absconded with the firm's stock-in-trade. Tyler recuperated from the financial difficulties brought about by the sudden disappearance of his former partner, and he continued to operate at 115 Canal Street, under his own name, until his death in 1879. E.A. Tyler's business was large and at one time or another employed a number of silversmiths. His firm manufactured and retailed silver in prevalent Victorian styles.

Tyler married Julia A. Barnes of Cambridge, Massachusetts. He belonged to the Mechanic Society of New Orleans, founded by Henry M. Dobbs. Tyler's loyalty to the Union was somewhat questionable during the Civil War. He was transported to Fort Jackson during the Federal occupation of New Orleans by General Benjamin Franklin "Spoons" Butler.

The firm of E.A. Tyler was succeeded by the jewelry business of George E. Strong at the same location, 115 Canal Street. This location was taken over in 1883 by Alvin M. Hill. Louis E. Tyler, son of Edward A. Tyler, was a clerk at George E. Strong's, and later worked for A.M. Hill. He finally formed his own business, E.A. Tyler's Son, in 1886 at 3 Camp Street. E.A. Tyler's Son was dissolved by syndic's sale in 1891.

E. A. Tyler. Wood engraving. Jewell, Edwin L. *Jewell's Crescent City Illustrated.* New Orleans, 1873. (The Historic New Orleans Collection)

E. A. Tyler advertisement. Jewell, Edwin. *Jewell's Crescent City Illustrated.* New Orleans, 1873. (The Historic New Orleans Collection)

102. Pair of Cups ca. 1848-1852

MARKS (on bottoms): "E. A. TYLER" in rectangle; "NEW ORLEANS" in rectangle.

DESCRIPTION: Cylindrical cups; lips with applied molding beading; applied molding at bases; applied, flared foot with band of palmette and string-and-ball motif on striated ground of each; simple loop handles. "M. C. HART" in script on side of left cup; "A. B. HART" in script on side of right cup.

MEASUREMENTS: LEFT: H. 9.5 cm (3³/₄ in); D. base 7.3 cm (2⁷/₈ in); W. 10.8 cm (4¹/₄ in); WT. 149.0 gm (4.79 oz) RIGHT: H. 10.2 cm (4 in); D. base 7.3 cm (2⁷/₈ in); W. 10.4 cm (4¹/₈ in); WT. 145.7 gm (4.68 oz)

PROVENANCE: Samuel M. Hart probably presented these cups to his two daughters: Margaret Clio Hart (1846-1898), later Mrs. David Gillihan, and Anna Belle Hart (1851-1916), later Mrs. Abner Lawson Duncan. Mrs. Duncan gave the pair to her niece, Mrs. John T. Anderson, Jr.

Anglo-American Art Museum 79.39.1-2
Louisiana State University
Baton Rouge, Louisiana
Gift of the Friends of the Museum

103. Cake Server ca. 1870

MARKS (on back of shoulder): "P", star symbol, "S" in circles; (on back of handle): "E. A. TYLER. N. O." incised, above partially rubbed; "STERLING" incised.

DESCRIPTION: Up curved, rounded handle; upper surface engraved with scrolls and flowers; twisted shank; trowel-shaped, pierced blade in diaper pattern with engraved floral and foliate border. "K" engraved in script on upper face of handle.

MEASUREMENTS: L. 26.2 cm (10⁵/₁₆ in); W. 7.5 cm (2¹⁵/₁₆ in); WT. 104.9 gm (3.37 oz)

The Historic New Orleans Collection 1979.373
New Orleans, Louisiana

The maker's marks are those of the partnership of Polhemus and Strong who worked in New York during the 1860s. John Polhemus patented the flatware which he supplied to a number of New Orleans silversmiths and jewelers. The word "STERLING" was added to the piece in 1978.

97

104. Creamer   ca. 1850

MARKS (on bottom of body): "E. A. TYLER" incised, above; "C. C. & D." in lozenge flanked by pseudo-hallmarks in ovals, above; "995" incised, above; "NEW ORLEANS" incised.

DESCRIPTION: Rococo-revival bulbous body; applied foliate band at lip and repeated upside down and reversed on vertical foot; chased grapevine, leaves, and grape clusters encircling neck; repoussé and chased scrolling foliage, flowers, "C"-scrolls, punchwork, and diapering around full part of body with "C"-scroll cartouche under spout; molded stepped base with reel shaft; naturalistic grapevine and scrolled handle with leaves and grape clusters. "B" engraved in script in cartouche.

MEASUREMENTS: H. 20.2 cm (7¹⁵/₁₆ in); D. base 8.0 cm (3¹/₈ in); W. 14.0 cm (5¹/₈ in); WT. 339.3 gm (10.90 oz)

PROVENANCE: The Blackburn family of New Orleans.

LOAN: *Private Collection*

"C.C. & D." has been attributed to Charters, Cann & Dunn, New York.

C. ROUYER

Pierre Casimir Rouyer was born in France in 1813. He arrived in New Orleans in 1849, and succeeded to the business of a Mr. Lefebure in 1850. When he moved his store from the corner of Royal and Dumaine Streets to 180 Chartres Street, between St. Peter and Jefferson, Rouyer advertised that he was a gilder and plater. He later moved to a variety of storefronts along Royal and Chartres Streets in the French Quarter.

In 1855, Rouyer advertised himself as a goldsmith, silversmith, and manufacturer of articles in bronze and other metals. He also imported silverplate from Charles Christofle of Paris, who had started his own plating industry after buying up existing French electroplate patents. Rouyer's pieces plus the many from Christofle gave him a large inventory, and among his clients were the principal restaurants and hotels of the city.

Rouyer also made various types of medals. These included the medal struck in 1860 to commemorate the dedication of the Henry Clay statue, and the P.G.T. Beauregard medal of 1861. Surviving examples of these have thus far remained unlocated.

In 1867, Rouyer's establishment was in liquidation. Rouyer's wife, Antoinette Heyl Rouyer, carried on the business until her death in 1886.

105. Skewer ca. 1855

MARKS (on upper part of shaft): "C. ROUYER" in rectangle, above; "D. L." incised.

DESCRIPTION: French silver plate; flat, tapered shaft with finial eagle, wings spread, head facing left, and perched on two-branch stump.

MEASUREMENTS: L. 27.3 cm (10¾ in); WT. 66.1 gm (2.13 ox)

LOAN: *Mr. Emile N. Kuntz*
New Orleans, Louisiana

Silver skewers are a rare form in American silver. This one differs from most modern skewers in that it has a flat blade rather than a rounded one. Particularly interesting is the cast eagle finial perched a top the blade. Each of the two dominant factions of the New Orleans populace in the mid-1800s would have had an affinity to such a symbolic motif. By that time the eagle had become a well-established symbol of American patriotism. And the French had also elevated the bird to a stately position during the Second Empire, then undergoing a revival in the United States.

Another silver skewer, also by Rouyer and almost identical to this one, is in the collection of the Louisiana State Museum, New Orleans.

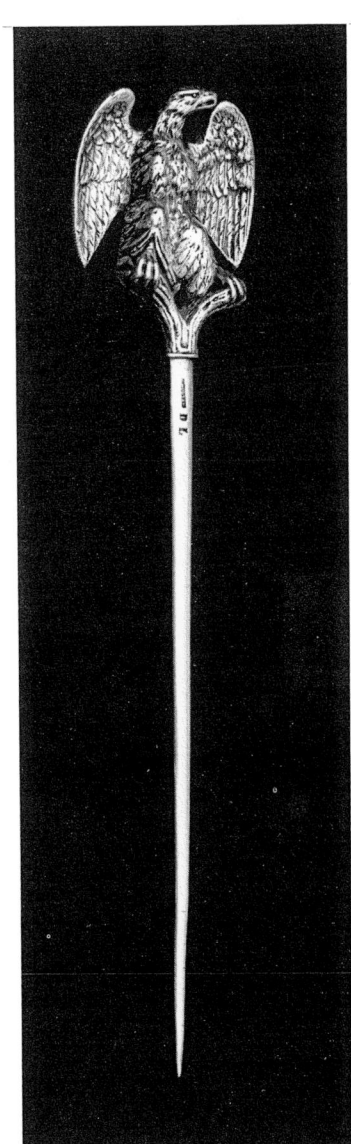

JOSEPH RAFEL

Joseph Rafel was born in Germany in 1810. He worked in New York and Cincinnati and came to New Orleans as an itinerant before moving his business there. In 1852, fire destroyed his store and the loan office he operated on St. Charles Street. His lost inventory included jewelry, clothing, musical instruments, surgical instruments, guns, and books. Fortunately, he was able to open another establishment soon after.

Rafel returned to New York during the Civil War. Following the conflict, his property on St. Charles Avenue between Jackson and Philip Streets was leased. In 1870, Rafel, then a permanent resident of New York, sold the cottage and land to Louisa Morgan Whitney, wife of Charles Augustus Whitney.

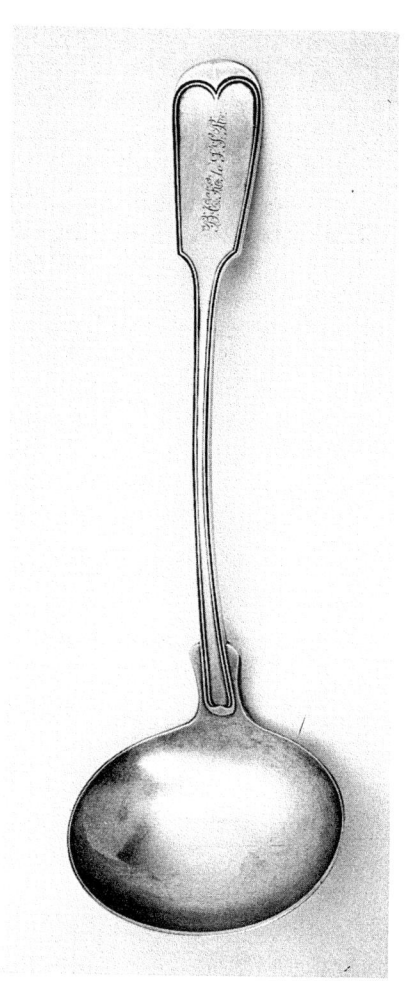

106. Ladle   ca. 1852-1861

MARK (on back of handle): "J. RAFEL. N.O." in rectangle.

DESCRIPTION: "Fiddle thread" handle; wavy shoulders; slightly flared oval bowl. "BCK to SSR" engraved in script on upper face of handle.

MEASUREMENTS: L. 33.3 cm (13⅛ in); D. bowl 10.5 cm (4⅛ in); WT. 194.1 gm (6.24 oz)

The Historic New Orleans Collection   1978.175.42
New Orleans, Louisiana

Joseph Rafel advertisement. *New Orleans Daily Delta,* 20 November 1866.

107. Goblet ca. 1852-1861

MARK (on bottom of bowl, on disc): "J. RAFEL. N.O." in arc.

DESCRIPTION: Bulbous body; Rococo-revival repoussé and chased foliage and flowers on bowl and on shoulder of foot; cartouche on side formed by scrolls and waves; beading just below flared lip; applied, domed base decorated with vertical palmette-and-dart band at foot.

MEASUREMENTS: H. 15.9 cm (6¼ in); D. lip 8.6 cm (3⅞ in); D. base 8.2 cm (3¼ in); WT. 223.1 gm (7.17 oz)

Anglo-American Art Museum 77.3.2
Louisiana State University
Baton Rouge, Louisiana
Gift of the Friends of the Museum

A similar foot appears in elongated form on a cup by Joseph Rafel (cat. no. 108).

108. Cup ca. 1852-1861

MARK (on bottom): "J. RAFEL. N.O." in arc.

DESCRIPTION: Cylindrical body terminating in rounded base on applied flared foot with palmette, string-and-ball motif against striated ground; repoussé cabbage roses and scrolling foliage on either side of Rococo-revival cartouche of "C"-scrolls and waves opposite the handle; beaded border just below lip and at juncture of bowl and foot; scroll handle with spurs. "PER" in script on side.

MEASUREMENTS: H. 8.9 cm (3½ in); D. lip 7.8 cm (3⅛ in); D. base 7.2 cm (2¹³⁄₁₆ in); W. 11.4 cm (4⅜ in); WT. 167.4 gm (5.38 oz)

Anglo-American Art Museum 79.16.12
Louisiana State University
Baton Rouge, Louisiana
Gift of Mrs. Rawlston D. Phillips, Sr.

H. P. BUCKLEY

Henry Peat Buckley was born in Coventry, England, 1822. He learned watchmaking in England and immigrated to the United States when he was about eighteen years old. In 1842, after living in New York almost three years, Buckley moved to New Orleans. Having established himself in the city he married Miss Caroline Beaumont of Coventry.

He was employed in New Orleans by the firm of Nelson A. Young, at 8 Camp Street. Nelson A. Young had been a partner of Edwin Whittemore in 1840, following the dissolution of Whittemore & Blair. After Young's death the business was managed by Young's widow until Buckley was taken in as a partner. About 1850, the firm title was changed to Young & Co., and eventually Buckley bought out the Young interest and operated the business under his own name. The firm of H.P. Buckley continued in the same location until Buckley's death in 1903. He was buried in the Masonic Cemetery in New Orleans.

H. P. Buckley. Wood engraving. *Cohen's New Orleans and Southern Directory for 1856.* New Orleans: Printed at the office of the Daily Delta, 1856. (The Historic New Orleans Collection)

H. P. Buckley store, Camp Street. Undated copy photograph from ca. 1890 original. (The Historic New Orleans Collection 1980.64)

H. P. Buckley advertisement. *Cohen's New Orleans Directory for 1855.* New Orleans: Printed at the office of the Picayune, 1855. (The Historic New Orleans Collection)

109. Cup ca. 1853

MARK (on bottom): "H. P. BUCKLEY" in rectangle.

DESCRIPTION: Octagonal body on conforming foot; cartouche of scrolling grapevines with grape clusters, opposite handle; molded lip with beading below; molded baseband above flared foot; scroll handle with spur thumbpiece. "A. B. Phelps/from her uncle/JDP/1st April 1853" engraved in script in cartouche.

MEASUREMENTS: H. 9.3 cm (3⅝ in); D. lip 7.9 cm (3⅛ in); D. base 8.5 cm (3⅜ in); W. 10.15 cm (4 in); WT. 174.5 gm (5.61 oz)

LOAN: *Estate of Mrs. Fred Reynaud, Sr. Houston, Texas*

This rather large cup was the baby cup of Ann Brown Phelps (1853-1857). In the twentieth century these cups are usually regarded as christening or baby cups, while during the Victorian period they were apparently used for all manner of presentations. An interesting example, also dating from 1853, is a cup made by Adolphe Himmel for presentation to a Dr. Moss as a gift from a patient following his recovery (cat. no. 43). Straight-sided, octagonal cups, while not common, were made in most American silversmithing centers, North and South, during the 1840s and 1850s.

110. Cup ca. 1879

MARKS (on bottom): "H. P. BUCKLEY" above; "N. ORLEANS" incised, partially rubbed.

DESCRIPTION: Cylindrical body; Rococo-revival reserve surrounded by "C"-scrolls, waves, scales, and flowers, opposite handle; beading below molded lip and on bold molded foot; double scroll handle with spur thumbpiece. "Sidney./from his/Godparents./April. 1879." engraved in script in reserve.

MEASUREMENTS: H. 8.9 cm (3½ in); D. lip 6.7 cm (2⅝ in); D. base 6.9 cm (2¹¹⁄₁₆ in); W. 9.9 cm (3¹⁵⁄₁₆ in); WT. 103.5 gm (3.33 oz)

The Historic New Orleans Collection 1978.175.19 New Orleans, Louisiana

GREGOR & WILSON

Gregor & Wilson was a partnership between George W. Gregor, John W. Gregor, and William A. Wilson, from 1856 to 1858. They were manufacturers and retailers who were located at the corner of Camp and Canal Streets.

Following the dissolution of the partnership, George W. Gregor formed a partnership with Rufus L. Bruce under the firm name of Gregor & Co., from 1858 to 1861.

William A. Wilson, said to have been "a gentleman of mild and kind description possessed of sterling virtues," was born in South Carolina in 1831. He continued to work in New Orleans until 1861.

Gregor & Wilson store, corner of Camp and Canal Streets. "Canal-Street, New Orleans," ca. 1856-1858 engraving by Louis Schwarz. (The Historic New Orleans Collection 1953.133.6)

111. Pair of Cups and Saucers   ca. 1856-1858

MARK (on bottom of cup bowl and bottom of saucer): "GREGOR & WILSON" incised.

DESCRIPTION: Bowl-shaped bodies; splayed foot with applied molding on each; leaf-chased scroll handles. "VFS" engraved monogram opposite handles and on cup rest in each saucer; applied at later date.

MEASUREMENTS: CUPS: H. each 5.4 cm (2¹/₈ in); D. lip each 7.6 cm (3 in); W. each 10.8 cm (4¹/₄ in); WTS. 93.6 gm (3.00 oz) SAUCERS: H. each 1.9 cm (³/₄ in); D. each 12.7 cm (5 in); WTS. 109.8 gm (3.53 oz)

The Historic New Orleans Collection   1979.370.1a,b-2a,b
New Orleans, Louisiana

P. ZIMMERMAN

The firm of P. Zimmermann was in operation in November of 1865, at 94 and 96 Canal Street, using the name of P. Zimmermann or just Zimmermann's. By December of 1866, P. Zimmermann had been succeeded or replaced by Charles H. Zimmermann.

P. Zimmermann advertised diamonds, watches, and spectacles for sale, and jewelry at wholesale. The firm also sold and manufactured silverware.

112. Cup ca. 1865

MARKS (on bottom): "P. ZIMMERMANN." in rectangle, above; "NEW ORLEANS" in rectangle.

DESCRIPTION: Cylindrical body; lip with applied molding and beading below; applied, molded baseband above applied vertical, foliated band as foot; double "C"-scroll handle with spur thumbpiece.

MEASUREMENTS: H. 9.8 cm (3⁷/₈ in); D.lip 7.0 cm (2³/₄ in); D. base 7.1 cm (2¹³/₁₆ in); W. 10.5 cm (4¹/₈ in); WT. 124.4 gm (4.00 oz)

LOAN: *Private Collection*

C. H. ZIMMERMAN

Charles H. Zimmermann either succeeded or replaced P. Zimmermann by December of 1866, when he advertised that his silverware factory was in order and open to the public. Zimmermann was an importer and manufacturer of fine jewelry, silverware, and plated ware at wholesale and retail. He was associated with Major William C. Driver, an experienced and accomplished silversmith formerly at Hyde & Goodrich.

In 1866, the store was described as having a wide range of table silverware, pitchers, teapots, goblets, and whatever article of use or ornament to be found on the tables of "refined and fashionable people."

The store closed in 1870, following the death of C. H. Zimmerman. His partner, W. C. Driver, died in New Orleans in 1874.

C. H. Zimmermann advertisement. *Gardner's New Orleans Directory for 1867.* New Orleans: Charles Gardner, 1867. (The Historic New Orleans Collection)

113. Cup   ca. 1866-1871

MARKS (on bottom): "C. H. ZIMMERMANN" incised, above; crescent moon with face, incised symbol, above; "NEW ORLEANS" incised.

DESCRIPTION: Urn-shaped body; applied flared lip band of stylized rosettes and brackets; applied, splayed foot with gadrooned edge; repoussé scroll cartouche and floral sprays; flat circular handle with ribbon-tied naturalistic stem terminating in three leaves at juncture with body. "JMM" engraved in script in cartouche.

MEASUREMENTS: H. 7.0 cm (2³/₄ in); D. lip 6.3 cm (2¹/₂ in); D base 4.7 cm (1⁷/₈ in); W. 8.5 cm (3⁹/₁₆ in); WT. 74.9 gm (2.41oz)

LOAN: *Katherine de M. Martinez*
New Orleans, Louisiana

114. Butter Cooler　　ca. 1870

MARKS (on bottom of bowl): "C. H. ZIMMERMANN" incised, above; crescent moon with face incised, above; "NEW ORLEANS" incised.

DESCRIPTION: Renaissance-revival three-part serving piece; round, footed bowl with flared rim, pierced liner, and domed lid; four cast medallions containing Neo-classical style profiles on lower part of lid; cast lamb finial as handle; edge of rim and applied cast foot of bowl with running border of oak leaves, arches, and bell flower on striated ground. "Helen/Dec. 1, 1870/from TLB" engraved in script on lid. Liner is a replacement.

MEASUREMENTS: H. 12.7 cm (4³/₄ in); D. base 7.8 cm (3¹/₈ in); W. 14.7 cm (5⁷/₈ in); WT. 367.6 gm (11.82 oz)

A. M. HILL

"A. M. Hill's Jewelry House, Canal Street," corner of Royal Street. Undated copy photograph. (The Vieux Carré Survey, Square 34, The Historic New Orleans Collection)

115. Pelican Pin   ca. 1884

MARK (on back): "A. M. HILL/NEW ORLEANS" incised.

DESCRIPTION: Gold-filled emblematic crescent-shaped mount, alligator support; Louisiana pelican on cotton bale. "NEW ORLEANS" on crescent.

MEASUREMENTS: H. 2.7 cm (1¹/₁₆ in); W. 2.4 cm (1 in); WT. 4.2 gm (.14 oz)

The Historic New Orleans Collection   1979.319
New Orleans, Louisiana

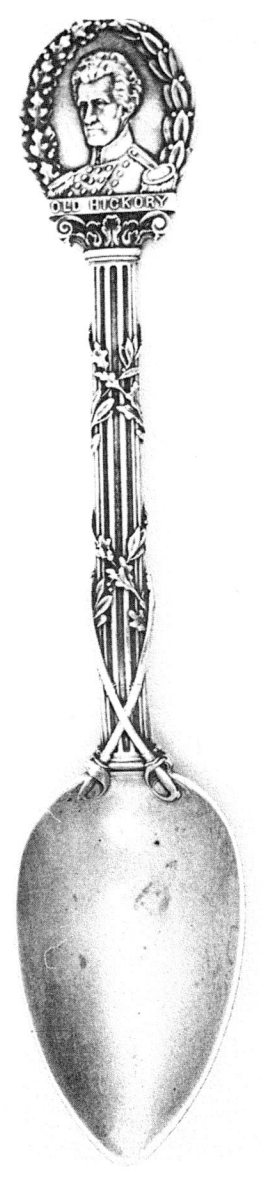

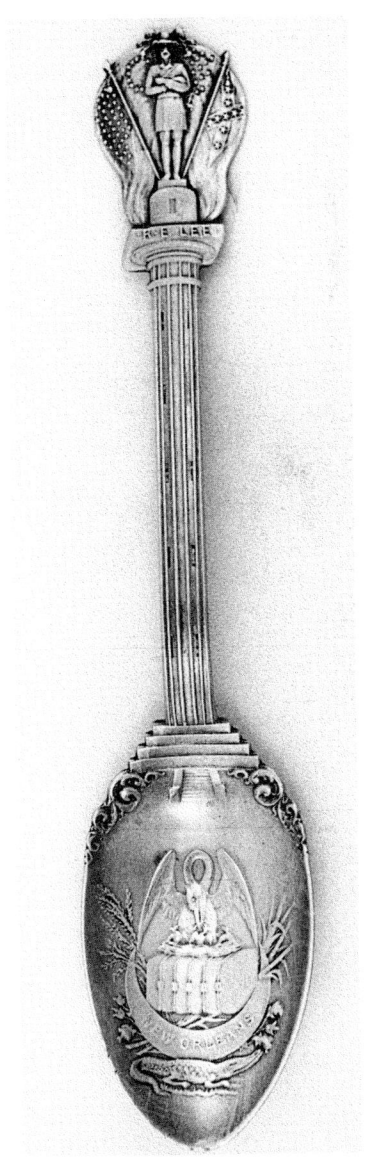

116. Souvenir Spoon   ca. 1891-1909

MARK (on back of bowl): "A. M. HILL/PAT. APRIL 25 '91/STERLING" incised.

DESCRIPTION: Teaspoon with words "Old Hickory" below bust of Andrew Jackson in oak-and-laurel-leaf wreath surmounting Corinthian column with cross bandings of oak-and-laurel; and crossed swords at base.

MEASUREMENTS: L. 15.4 cm (6¹/₁₆ in); WT. 32.5 gm (1.04 oz)

LOAN: *Private Collection*

117. Souvenir Spoon   ca. 1891-1909

MARK (on back of bowl): "A. M. HILL/PAT. APRIL 25 '91/STERLING" incised.

DESCRIPTION: Teaspoon with Robert E. Lee flanked by flags of Confederate States of America above Ionic column; bowl ornamented with Louisiana pelican, cotton bale, crescent, alligator, and foliage indigenous to Louisiana.

MEASUREMENTS: L. 15.2 cm (6 in); WT. 29.6 gm (.95 oz)

LOAN: *Mr. and Mrs. William Christovich New Orleans, Louisiana*

118- Souvenir Spoons (Demitasse, Teaspoon, Orange)
120. ca. 1900

MARKS (on back of handle): "D" script, in circle, to left of "STERLING/PAT'D/M. SCOOLER" incised.

DESCRIPTION: Rounded, oval up curved handle with pelican, cotton bale, and cane handle on front. "NEW ORLEANS, LA." raised on reverse. "Rex" and crown engraved in bowl; "T J J/1900" engraved in script on back of bowl (of orange spoon only).

MEASUREMENTS: DEMITASSE: L. 10.6 cm (4³/₁₆ in); WT. 11.4 gm (.37 oz) TEASPOON: L. 14.6 cm (5³/₄ in); WT. 28.9 gm (.93 oz) ORANGE: L. 15.0 cm (5⁷/₈ in); WT. 28.7 gm (.92 oz)

LOAN: *Private Collections*

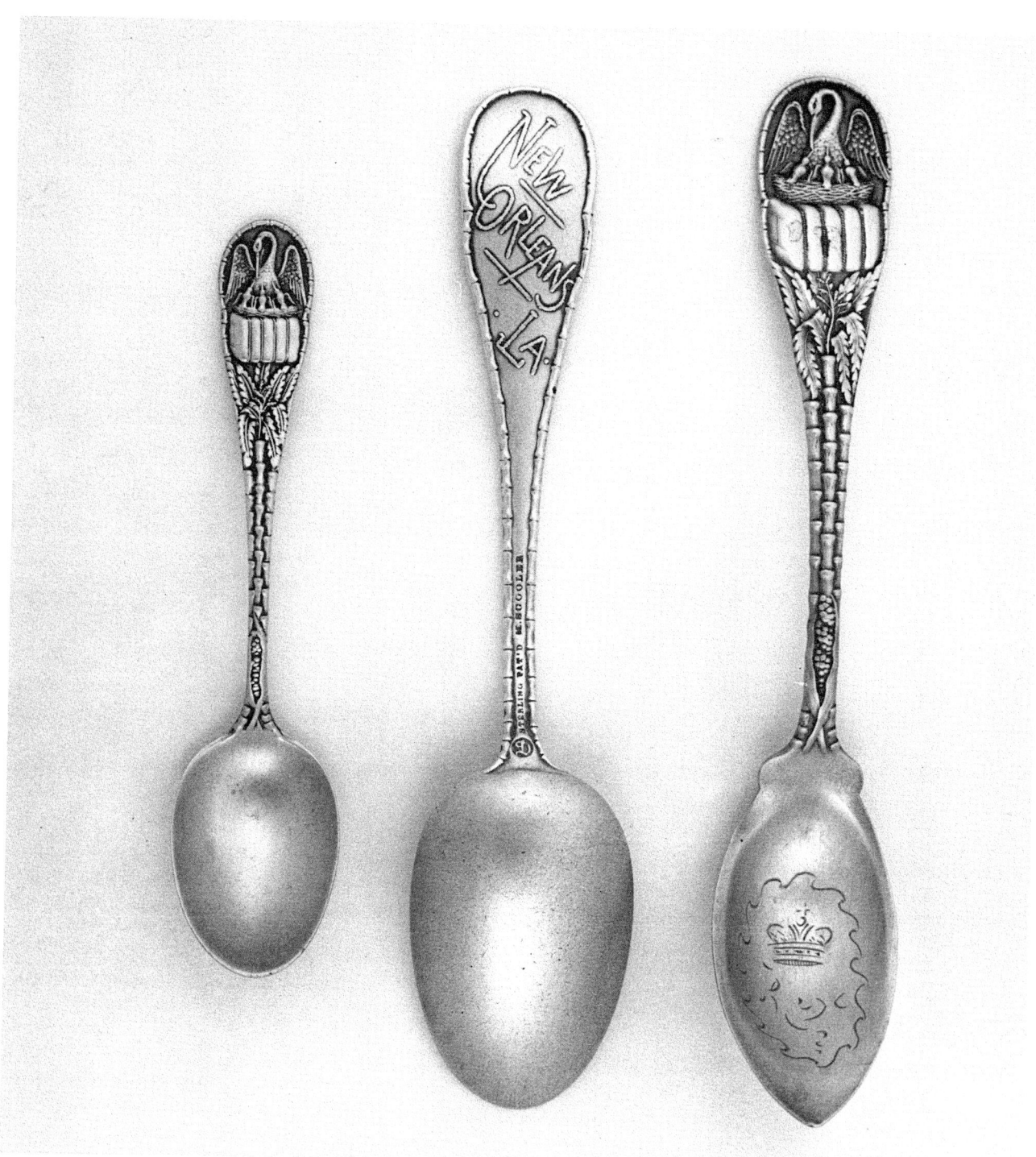

LOAN: (top row, left to right) 121. *Private Collection* 122. *The Historic New Orleans Collection* 123-126. *Private Collections*

(bottom row, left to right) 127. *The Historic New Orleans Collection* 128. *Private Collection* 129. *Mr. and Mrs. William Christovich, New Orleans, Louisiana* 130. *Private Collection* 131-132 *The Historic New Orleans Collection* 133-135. *Private Collections*

In the late nineteenth century, a multitude of patterns for silver spoon handles were mass-produced by large commercial silver companies. The well-traveled American public became enamored with collecting souvenir spoons from American cities and states. The spoons were made in several sizes with the majority being coffee (or demitasse), tea, and orange spoons (cat. nos. 118-120).

In New Orleans, the earliest souvenir spoons were probably associated with the World's Industrial and Cotton Centennial Exposition held in 1884-1885, on the present site of Audubon Park (cat. no. 127). This and all the spoons that followed (cat. nos. 116-135) were specialty items made in the northeast by firms such as Górham Company of Providence, Rhode Island (cat. nos. 123, 127, 131); William B. Durgin Co. of Concord, New Hamp-

shire (cat. nos. 118-120); and Watson, Newell & Co., 1879-1905 (cat. nos. 122, 129, 130), or Watson Co., after 1910 (cat. nos. 124, 133, 135), of Attleboro, Massachusetts.

Since such flatware required completely different machinery, tools, and production from those used in making hollowware, the large companies manufactured and exported designs specifically oriented to a local market. The fronts and backs of the handles and the bowls of the spoons were decorated with themes of important events, national heroes, street scenes, buildings, monuments, and city and state emblems. Three surviving examples illustrate the patented designs of New Orleans silversmiths, although the items themselves were manufactured in New York where the special equipment was available.

GLOSSARY

ACANTHUS LEAF A form of ornamentation patterned on the leaf of a prickly herb which is native to the Mediterranean region—chiefly the form of the leaf used in the Corinthian order capital (see cat. no. 41).

APPLIED Parts of a piece of silverware that are fabricated separately and applied with solder. Handles, spouts, covers, feet, and finials are common examples of separately made parts (see cat. nos. 2, 3, 6).

ANTHEMION A classical, stylized honeysuckle decoration which is usually employed as a band of consecutive anthemia or alternating with other Classical motifs (see cat. no. 12).

BEADING A decorative border composed of small, contiguous half-spheres (see cat. nos. 2, 3).

"C"-SCROLL The letter "C" used as a decorative motif either raised or engraved. "C"-scrolls are commonly found on Rococo-revival silverware. Cartouches and reserves are frequently formed by "C"-scrolls (see cat. no. 5).

CARTOUCHE A panel, tablet, or scroll created by embossing or engraving a border, and whose plane or convex reserve thus formed can be ornamented with a monogram, inscription, or date (see cat. no. 15).

CAST An object formed by molten silver being poured into a mold as opposed to an object being fashioned from sheet silver. Handles, finials, and ornaments are frequently cast (see cat. nos. 32, 42).

CHASING Relief decoration raised by surface hammering of the metal. The term is also applied to the finishing given to cast or repoussé work. In the former case, roughness or projections may be filed or cut away (see REPOUSSÉ) (see cat. no. 37).

COIN SILVER Silver composed of roughly 900/1000 parts of fine or pure silver to 100/1000 parts of alloy. The words COIN, PURE COIN, DOLLAR, STANDARD, and the letters C and D were marks used to indicate coin silver. This standard was being employed by good New Orleans silversmiths as late as the 1870s (see cat. nos. 32, 55).

CONTINENTAL MANNER Silverware made in designs favored by continental Europeans, especially the French, as opposed to objects made in the English taste (see cat. nos. 26, 79).

CURULE-AND-CROSS BORDER A border design whose principal motif is two co-joining ellipses which resemble the curving legs of an ancient Roman campstool. Each curule motif is separated from the next by a small Gothic-revival cross (see cat. no. 44).

CRENELLATED A type of border that resembles the medieval battlement type parapet in architecture, *i.e.* the top edge is alternately and uniformly depressed (see cat. no. 19).

CIPHER MONOGRAM An interweaving of letters to form a monogram—frequently a double monogram (see cat. nos. 62, 63).

DIAPER Ornament composed of small squares or lozenges forming an overall pattern (see cat. no. 10).

EMBOSSING A general term used to describe relief work on metals. The term formerly applied only to hammered work.

ENGINE TURNING The engraving of symmetrical patterns on metals by machinery. These patterns can be decorative or can be the utilitarian marks of a spinning machine used to raise a vessel (see cat. no. 46).

ENGRAILED Ornamenting with a pattern indented on the edge. This term is usually employed in relation to silverware to describe the border on the recessed cartouche of a maker's mark. It is interchangeable with SERRATED (see cat. no. 78).

ENGRAVING Mechanically cut lines in metal made with a graver or scorper (see cat. nos. 21, 45).

FLARED Basically the widening of a tubular form; funnel-like. Frequently used to describe the configuration of a foot or rim in hollowware (see cat. no. 38).

GADROON A hammered or cast border ornament composed of radiating flutes or reeds of curved or straight form. This border is used principally on the lips and feet of drinking vessels and on the edges of dishes and plates (see cat. nos. 56, 84).

GUILLOCHE An ornamental border of Classical origin consisting of two continuous intersecting ribbons which form a succession of circles or ovals (see cat. no. 59).

MOLDING or MOLDED BORDER Describing a simple decorative band which can project or be incised or both. The projecting molding is usually convex and the incised molding is concave.

PALMETTE An ornamental border based on the formalized palm leaf. In its classical sense there are usually several palm leaves creating a fanlike motif. As a border on New Orleans-made silver, it is a continuous border of vertical palm leaves on a striated ground, each separated from the other by a string-and-ball motif (see cat. nos. 38, 65).

PSEUDO-HALLMARKS Devices used principally by east coast American silversmiths to suggest that their wares were manufactured from fine quality silver. All British-made silverware had to be tested by official government assay offices to determine that it was sterling standard or above before it could be hallmarked and retailed (see cat. no. 21).

PUNCHWORK Decorative designs made by a figured die called a puncheon. In silverware, punchwork is usually a pattern of indentations used as a background for a more important decorative motif (see cat. no. 20).

RAISED Refers to the technique of forming the body of a piece of hollowware from a flat circle of silver. The sheet of silver is hammered in concentric circles over a series of anvils with frequent annealing (see cat. no. 67).

REPOUSSÉ Relief ornament that is hammered from the under or inner side of silver or other metals. Sharpness of form is usually given by surface chasing of detail and outline (see cat. no. 54).

RESERVE A cartouche that is formed on a piece of silver either by engraving, repoussé work, or casting. The blank area thus formed can be embellished with a coat of arms, scene, monogram, or presentation inscription (see cat. no. 37).

RINCEAUX   A stylized ornament, usually in low relief, consisting of scrolling stems with stiff, acanthus leaves which is derived from Classical Roman architecture (see cat. no. 52).

ROCOCO-REVIVAL   A nineteenth-century decorative style using the vocabulary of the early eighteenth-century French "rocaille" style. However, cabriole legs, "S"- and "C"-scrolls, shell carvings, and curvilinear surfaces were employed in new materials with the techniques of the new machine age in the fabrication of furniture, silver, textiles, and ceramics. The product was heavier in both overall configuration and decoration. The Rococo-revival did not have wide appeal in American silver until the 1840s when hollowware made from then and through to the 1860s frequently displayed a riot of repoussé foliage, floral, fruit, and animal motifs, and sentimental scenes (see cat. no. 36).

SCALLOPED   A type of continuous border employing ellipses and appearing like the edge of a shell (see cat. no. 14).

SEAMED SHEET SILVER   A constructional technique by which a flat sheet of silver is raised or bent together to form a vessel. The joining ends of the modeled piece of silver are soldered together on a seam which can be detected by careful examination even in well-finished pieces (see cat. no. 97).

SERRATED   A notched or toothed edge, like the blade on a saw.

Used in connection with silverware chiefly to describe the border edging a recessed cartouche around a smith's mark.

SPLAYED   The foot of a cup, goblet, pitcher, or other vessel is termed splayed when the top and bottom diameters are different (see cat. no. 3).

STERLING   The standard of 925/1000 parts of fine silver, with 75/1000 of added alloy (usually copper) to give it strength and stiffness, was established in England during the reign of Elizabeth I. The United States government did not require that this standard be employed on all pieces marked "sterling" until the Stamping Act of 1906. Baltimore-made silver employed the standard as early as 1800. It comes into general American usage after 1860 (see cat. nos. 61, 62).

TROY WEIGHT   A system of measurement commonly used in England and the United States for weighing precious metals—named after Troyes, France. A troy ounce equals 20 pennyweights (dwt.) and there are 12 ounces in a troy pound. One troy ounce equals 31.103 grams and is the conversion factor used in this catalogue.

VITRUVIAN SCROLL or WAVE   Border ornamentation of Classical origin composed of a band of convoluted scrolls.

WRIGGLEWORK   A form of engraved decoration that is wormlike in the way it moves to and fro (see cat. no. 93).

BIBLIOGRAPHY

Among the sources consulted by the authors and not cited in the text of the catalogue are the following: *Louisiana Supreme Court Reports; Louisiana Reports; Martin's Reports* (old and new series); *McGloin's Unreported Cases; Louisiana Annual Reports; United States Census Records for Louisiana* (1805-1870); New Orleans Board of Health death certificates (1818-1915); New Orleans city directories (1805-1932); New Orleans notarial archives; and city and parish cemetery records.

The authors also used contemporary accounts reported in the following New Orleans newspapers: *L'Abeille, Commercial Bulletin, Daily Advertiser, Daily Creole, Daily Crescent City, Daily Delta, Daily Orleanian, Daily Picayune, Daily States, Daily Times, Daily Tropic, Daily True Delta, Democrat, Deutzche Zeitung, The Era, Gazette de la Louisiane, Item, The Jefferson, Lafayette City Advertiser, Louisiana Advertiser, Louisiana Courier, Louisiana Gazette, Mercantile Advertiser, Le Moniteur de la Louisiane, Price Current and Commercial Intelligence, States, Times, Tribune, Times-Democrat, Times-Picayune, True Democrat, The Union.*

The American Tradition in Gold and Silver. Miami: Lowe Art Museum, University of Miami, 1975.

Arthur, Stanley Clisby, and Kernion, George Campbell Huchet de, eds. *Old Families of Louisiana.* 1931. Reprint. Baton Rouge: Claitor's, 1971.

Arthur, Stanley Clisby. *Old New Orleans: A History of the Vieux Carré, Its Ancient and Historical Buildings.* New Orleans: Harmanson, 1936.

Avery, C. Louise. *The Metropolitan Museum of Art: American Silver of the XVII and XVIII Century: A Study Based on the Clearwater Collection.* New York: Gillis Press, 1920.

Bacot, H. Parrott. *The Louisiana Landscape 1800-1969.* Baton Rouge: Anglo-American Art Museum, Louisiana State University, 1969.

Bacot, H. Parrott. *Southern Furniture and Silver: The Federal Period, 1788-1830.* Baton Rouge: Anglo-American Art Museum, Louisiana State University, 1968.

Bacot, H. Parrott, and Lambdin, Bethany. *Nineteenth Century Natchez-Made Silver.* Baton Rouge: Anglo-American Art Museum, Louisiana State University, 1970.

Beckman, Elizabeth D. *Cincinnati Silversmiths, Jewelers, Watch and Clockmakers.* Harrison, N.Y.: R.A. Green, 1975.

Belden, Gail, and Snodin, Michael. *Collecting for Tomorrow, Spoons.* Radnor, Pa.: Chilton, 1976.

Bloomsfield-Moore, Clara Sophie. *Sensible Etiquette of the Best Society, Customs, Manners, Morals and Home Culture.* Philadelphia: Porter and Coates, 1878.

Boutet de Monvel, Louis Maurice. *La Civilité Puérile et Honnête, Expliquée par L'Oncle Eugène et Illustrée par M. B. de Monvel.* Paris: Plon-Nourret, n.d.

Brillat-Savarin, Jean A. *Physiology of Taste.* 1825. Reprint. New York: Liveright, 1948.

Bruns, Mrs. Thomas Nelson Carter, comp. *Louisiana Portraits.* New Orleans: National Society of the Colonial Dames of America in the State of Louisiana, 1975.

Buhler, Kathryn C. *American Silver 1655-1825 in the Museum of Fine Arts, Boston.* Boston: Museum of Fine Arts, 1972.

Buhler, Kathryn, and Hood, Graham. *American Silver: Garvan and Other Collections in the Yale University Art Gallery.* New Haven, Conn.: Yale University Press, 1970.

Burton, E. Milby. *South Carolina Silversmiths 1690-1860.* Charleston: Charleston Museum, 1968.

Cable, George W. *The Creoles of Louisiana.* London: J. C. Nimmo, 1885.

Carey, Mary Sada. "The History of Table Manners and Customs and Influence Upon Manners and Customs of South Louisiana." Master's Thesis, Louisiana State University, 1933.

Carpenter, Charles H., and Carpenter, Mary Grace. *Tiffany Silver.* New York: Dodd, Mead, 1978.

Castellanos, Henry C. *New Orleans As It Was.* 1895. Reprint. Baton Rouge: Louisiana State University Press, 1978.

Checklist for Exhibition of Early Southern Made Furniture, Silver and Paintings. Baton Rouge: Anglo-American Art Museum, Louisiana State University, 1975.

Clark, John G. *New Orleans, 1718-1812: An Economic History.* Baton Rouge: Louisiana State University Press, 1970.

Cochran, Estelle M. Fortier. *The Fortier Family, and Allied Families.* San Antonio, 1963.

Coleman, William Head, comp. *Historical Sketch Book and Guide to New Orleans and Environs.* New York: W.H. Coleman, 1885.

Currier, Ernest M. *Marks of Early American Silversmiths.* Portland, Me.: Southworth Anthoesen Press, 1938.

Curtis, Nathaniel Cortlandt. *New Orleans: Its Old Houses, Shops and Public Buildings.* Philadelphia: J. B. Lippincott, 1933.

Cutten, George Barton. *Silversmiths of North Carolina 1696-1850.* Raleigh: Department of Cultural Resources, Division of Archives and History, 1973.

Davis, Edwin Adams. *Louisiana: A Narrative History.* 3d ed. Baton Rouge: Claitor's, 1971.

The Decorative Arts Society Newsletter. V (September 1979).

Designs for Gold and Silversmiths. London: Ackerman, 1836.

Dufour, Charles L., and Huber, Leonard V. If Ever I Cease to Love; One Hundred Years of Rex, 1872-1971. New Orleans: School of Design, 1970.

Editors of the Pyne Press, comp. Victorian Silverplated Hollowware. Princeton: Pyne Press, 1972.

Ensko, Stephen G. C. American Silversmiths and Their Marks II. New York: R. Ensko, 1937.

Fales, Martha Gandy. Early American Silver for the Cautious Collector. New York: Funk and Wagnalls, 1970.

Fitzpatrick, John. The Merchant of Manchac: The Letterbooks of John Fitzpatrick, 1768-1790. Edited by Margaret Fisher Dalrymple. Baton Rouge: Louisiana State University Press, 1978.

Flynt, Henry N., and Fales, Martha Gandy. The Heritage Collection of Silver, Old Deerfield, Massachusetts. Deerfield, Mass.: Heritage Foundation, 1968.

Foley, Helen. Harrod Silver Collection: A Gallery Leaflet; The Isaac Delgado Museum of Art, City Park, New Orleans, La. New Orleans: Louisiana Works Progress Administration, Delgado Museum of Art Project, 1937.

Fortier, Alcée. A History of Louisiana. New York: Manzi, Joyant, 1904.

Fossier, Albert E. New Orleans: The Glamour Period, 1800-1840. New Orleans: Pelican, 1957.

French, Hollis. A Silver Collector's Glossary and a List of Early American Silversmiths and Their Marks. New York: Da Capo, 1967.

Friends of the Cabildo, New Orleans. 250 Years of Life in New Orleans. New Orleans: Louisiana State Museum, 1968.

Gayarré, Charles. History of Louisiana. 1854-1866. Reprint. Gretna, La.: Pelican, 1974.

Gibbs, James W. Dixie Clockmakers. Gretna, La.: Pelican, 1979.

Gourley, Hugh. The New England Silversmith: An Exhibition of New England Silver from the Mid-Seventeenth Century to the Present Selected from New England Collections. Providence: Museum of Art, Rhode Island School of Design, 1965.

Green, Robert Alan. Marks of American Silversmiths. Harrison, N.Y.: R.A. Green, 1977.

Harmon, Nolan B. The Famous Case of Myra Clark Gaines. Baton Rouge: Louisiana State University Press, 1946.

Hayden, Arthur. Chats on Old Silver. 1905. Reprint. New York: Dover, 1969.

Holland, John A. A Treatise on the Progressive Improvement and Present State of the Manufactures in Metal. London: Longmann, Brown, Green and Longmann, 1831-1834.

Holland, Margaret. Phaidon Guide to Silver. Oxford: Phaidon Press, 1978.

Hood, Graham. American Silver, A History of Style, 1650-1900. New York: Praeger, 1971.

Hoopes, Penrose R. Connecticut Clockmakers of the Eighteenth Century. New York: Dover, 1974.

Huber, Leonard V. New Orleans: A Pictorial History. New York: Crown, 1971.

Jackson, Joy J. New Orleans in the Gilded Age: Politics and Urban Progress, 1880-1896. Baton Rouge: Published by Louisiana State University Press for the Louisiana Historical Association, 1969.

Jewell, Edwin L., ed. Jewell's Crescent City Illustrated. New Orleans, 1873.

Kauffman, Henry J. The Colonial Silversmith, His Technique and His Products. New York: Galahad, 1969.

Kendall, John Smith. History of New Orleans. Chicago: Lewis, 1922.

King, Grace. Creole Families of New Orleans. 1921. Reprint. Baton Rouge: Claitor's, 1971.

King, Grace. New Orleans: The Place and the People. New York: Macmillan, 1922.

Kirkland, Caroline Mathilda. The Evening Book on Fireside Talk on Morals and Manners with Sketches of Western Life. New York: Scribner, 1853.

Korn, Bertram Wallace. The Early Jews of New Orleans. Waltham, Mass.: American Jewish Historical Society, 1969.

Kovel, Ralph M., and Kovel, Terry H. A Directory of American Silver, Pewter and Silver Plate. New York: Crown, 1961.

La Cour, Arthur Burton, and Landry, Stuart Omer. New Orleans Masquerade. 2d ed. New Orleans: Pelican, 1957.

Landry, Stuart O. History of the Boston Club. New Orleans: Pelican, 1938.

Leslie, Eliza. The Behaviour Book: A Manual for Ladies. 4th ed. Philadelphia: Hayard, 1853.

Louisiana State Museum, New Orleans. Louisiana State Museum, New Orleans. Handbook of Information Concerning Its Historic Buildings and the Treasures They Contain. By Robert Glenk. New Orleans: Louisiana State Museum, 1934.

McClinton, Katharine Morrison. Collecting American 19th Century Silver. New York: Scribner, 1968.

Martin, Francois-Xavier. The History of Louisiana. 1827-1829. Reprint. Gretna, La.: Pelican, 1975.

May, Earl Chapin. Century of Silver, 1847-1948: Connecticut Yankees and a Noble Metal. New York: R.T. McBride, 1947.

Miceli, Augusto P. The Pickwick Club of New Orleans. New Orleans: Pickwick Press, 1964.

Murphy, Claudia Quigley. The History of the Art of Tablesetting, Ancient and Modern, from Anglo-Saxon Days to the Present Time. New York: DeVinne, 1921.

Museum of Fine Arts, Houston. "A Gift of Southern Silver." Bulletin 3 (April 1972): 19-20.

O'Connor, Thomas, ed. History of the Fire Department of New Orleans. New Orleans, 1895.

Owen, William Miller. In Camp and Battle with the Washington Artillery of New Orleans. Boston: Ticknor, 1885.

Pleasants, Jacob Hall, and Sill, Howard. *Maryland Silversmiths 1715-1830.* Harrison, N.Y.: R.A. Green, 1972.

Rainwater, Dorothy T. *Encyclopedia of American Silver Manufacturers.* New York: Crown, 1975.

Reinders, Robert C. *End of an Era: New Orleans, 1850-1860.* New Orleans: Pelican, 1964.

Rightor, Henry. *Standard History of New Orleans, Louisiana.* Chicago: Lewis, 1900.

Ripley, Eliza. *Social Life in Old New Orleans: Being Recollections of My Girlhood.* New York: Appleton, 1912.

Roach, Ruth H. *St. Louis Silversmiths.* St. Louis, Mo.: Eden, 1977.

Robin, Claude C. *Voyage to Louisiana, 1803-1805.* New Orleans: Pelican, 1966.

Saxon, Lyle. *Old Louisiana.* 1929. Reprint. New Orleans: R. L. Crager, 1950.

"Second Loan Collection of Old Silver Gathered from Homes of New Orleans." *Bulletin of the Isaac Delgado Museum of Art,* vol. 3, no. 3 (February 1939).

Sedgwick, Catherine Maria. *Morals of Manners; or, Hints for Our Young People.* New York: Putnam, 1846.

Seebold, Herman de Bachelle. *Old Louisiana Plantation Homes and Family Trees.* 1941. Reprint. Gretna, La.: Pelican, 1971.

Smith, Sidney Adair. *Mobile Silversmiths and Jewelers 1820-1867.* Mobile, Ala.: Historic Mobile Preservation Society, 1970.

Soards' Blue Book of New Orleans, for 1890/91. New Orleans: L. Soards, 1890.

Southern Silver, An Exhibition of Silver Made in the South Prior to 1860; September 27/November 10, 1968. Houston: Museum of Fine Arts, 1968.

Sterling Silver Hollowware. Introduction by Dorothy T. Rainwater. Princeton: Pyne Press, 1973.

Stillinger, Elizabeth. *The Antiques Guide to Decorative Arts in America 1600-1875.* New York: Dutton, 1973.

Tardy. *Les Poinçoins de Garantie Internationaux pour l'Argent.* 12th ed. Paris: 1942.

Tracy, Berry B. *Nineteenth-Century America: Furniture and Other Decorative Arts.* New York: Metropolitan Museum of Art, 1970.

Trollope, Anthony. *North America.* London: Chapman and Hall, 1866.

Trollope, Frances. *Domestic Manners of the Americans.* London: Whittacker, Teacher, 1832.

Ward, Barbara McLean, and Ward, Gerald W., eds. *Silver in American Life: Selections from the Mabel Brady Garvan and Other Collections at Yale University.* New York: American Federation of Arts, 1979.

Warren, David B. *Bayou Bend: American Furniture, Paintings and Silver from the Bayou Bend Collection.* Houston: Museum of Fine Arts, 1975.

Warren, David B. *Southern Silver: An Exhibition of Silver Made in the South Prior to 1860.* Houston: Museum of Fine Arts, 1968.

Wyler, Seymour B. *The Book of Old Silver.* New York: Crown, 1937.

Young, Perry. *The Mistick Krewe.* 1931. Reprint. New Orleans: Louisiana Heritage Press, 1969.

NEW ORLEANS SILVER
IN PUBLIC COLLECTIONS

Anglo-American Art Museum
Louisiana State University
Baton Rouge, Louisiana

Cooper-Hewitt Museum
The Smithsonian Institution's
    National Museum of Design
New York, New York

The Historic New Orleans Collection
New Orleans, Louisiana

Louisiana State Museum
New Orleans, Louisiana

The Museum of Fine Arts
Houston, Texas
The Bayou Bend Collection

New Orleans Museum of Art
New Orleans, Louisiana

The Wadsworth Atheneum
Hartford, Connecticut

The Henry Francis duPont Winterthur Museum
Winterthur, Delaware

Yale University Art Gallery
New Haven, Connecticut

NEW ORLEANS SILVERSMITHS

This list has been compiled from New Orleans city directories, newspapers, civil and ecclesiastical records, and family documents. The list by no means contains all of the silver workers and retailers active in New Orleans. The authors do feel, however, that the most important individuals and firms ranging from the eighteenth century to the early 1900s have been noted.

The entries in the listing are of two types. One is for an individual craftsman. The first line lists the name of the person (last name first), and his life span. In some instances, the first name is entirely missing, or only indicated by an initial. Life spans for these craftsmen were often unknown, and sometimes only a birth or death date is known. These are preceded by b. or d. If the individual was known by other names, these are also shown. On following lines are: the occupation of the craftsman and his active dates; and apprenticeships or associations with firms, followed by the dates for those associations.

The second type of entry is one for a business establishment. The name of the firm is shown on the first line. Successive lines list the names of the major partners in the firm; the type of business and dates of operation; successions of the business. Where information is incomplete or not applicable, all of the above information will not be listed in each entry.

ADAM, Hilaire
Goldsmith: 1811-1817

ADAM, Jean B.
Goldsmith and Gardener: 1811-1830

ADLER, Coleman E. (1868-1938)
Jeweler: 1898-1933

AMY, Pierre (1765-1824)
Goldsmith: 1811-1824

ANDERSON, James D.
Importer of watches and jewelry: 1849-1853

ANGLAIRE, Joseph
Goldsmith and Jeweler: 1827-1853

ANTZ, B.
Goldsmith and Jeweler: 1849

ANTZ, Ernest
Silversmith: 1880

ANTZ, George
Silversmith and Engraver: 1838-1854

ARANS, Joseph (b. 1782)
Silversmith: 1822

ARCHARD, Antoine
Goldsmith: 1811

ARCHAUD, Pierre (Also AR-CHARD and HACHARD)
Goldsmith: 1822-1830

ARNAUD, J.B.
Goldsmith and Watchmaker: 1813-1826

AUOCULI, J.
Goldsmith: 1838

AVINENC, Candide (1804-1861)
Goldsmith and Jeweler: 1832-1861

AVRIL, Hugues (1776-1842)
Goldsmith and Jeweler: 1811-1832

A. BALDWIN & CO.
Hardware and Cutlery: 1860-1894

A. BALDWIN & CO., LTD.
Hardware and Cutlery: 1895-1927

A. BALDWIN & CO., INC.
Hardware: after 1928

H.E. BALDWIN & CO.
(Horace E. Baldwin)
Jeweler: 1842-1853

BALIX, Paul (free man of color)
Goldsmith: 1849-1850

BARBARET, Simeon Theon
Goldsmith: 1811

BARBARET, Theon
Guns and Goldsmith: 1817-1830

BARELLE, F.
Goldsmith: 1832

BASTID, Joseph
Goldsmith, Jeweler, and Watchmaker: 1822-1827

BASTIEN, Joseph
Jeweler and Goldsmith: 1822-1823

BAUMANN, August
Watchmaker and Jeweler: 1862-1932

BAYSSET, Joseph M. (1796-1866)
Goldsmith: 1822-1827

BELLANGAME, Misse
Goldsmith: 1821

BELLANGER, Jean P.
Goldsmith and Jeweler: 1810-1827

BELLIARD, Francois (b. 1787)
Goldsmith: 1820-1835
With Ville & Belliard: 1823-1835

BELLO, Pierre (1781-1824)
Goldsmith, Watchmaker, Optician and Philosophical Glass Blower: 1824

BELLOME, Gregoire
Goldsmith: 1830

BERMINGHAM, Henry (b. 1904)
Silversmith: 1917-1950

BERNIARD, Jules (b. 1844)
Jeweler: 1860-1872

BERNIARD, Leopold (1814-1883)
Jeweler: 1841-1870

BERNIARD, Louis (b. 1812)
Jeweler: 1855-1869

BERTIN, Pierre
Goldsmith

BIDAULT, Etienne
Goldsmith: 1813

BIDOLE, Thomas
Goldsmith: 1824-1827

BIDOT, Jean-Baptiste (1702-1725)
Goldsmith

BIER, Seikman (b. 1822)
Jeweler: 1860-1870

BIRTEL, Frank G.
Silversmith: 1880-1912
With T. Hausmann: 1880-1882
With John Maikell: 1883
With Emile Graeser: 1890-1891

BITTER, Henry
Goldsmith: 1849

BLAIR, Daniel
St. Louis: 1817-1820s
New Orleans: 1830-1842
With Harland & Blair: 1830-1833
With Hazard & Blair: 1834
With Whittemore & Blair: 1838-1840
With Blair & Lawes: 1840

BLAIR & LAWES
(Daniel Blair and Lawes)
Jewelry: 1840-1842

BLANCHOIN,
Goldsmith: 1817

BLISS, H. (d 1830)
Silversmith
With Harland & Bliss: 1830

BLISS, John
Watchmaker: 1830-1834
With Bliss & Whittemore: 1833-1834

BLISS & WHITTEMORE
(John Bliss and Edwin Whittemore)
Jewelry: 1833-1835

BOISDORE, Louis
Goldsmith: 1828

BOISSECQ, Jules
Gunsmith: 1842

BONJEAN, Victor Amedee (1766-1831)
Goldsmith: 1822-1830

BONNET, Adrien (b. 1835)
Jeweler: 1861-1872

BONNET & CO.
(Adrien Bonnet)
Jewelry:
Succeeded by Frantz & Opitz in 1879

BOUJOU, Joseph
Jeweler:
1807-1809 (New Orleans)
1812-1849 (St. Louis)

BOWLES & JUDSON
Silver Plate Workers: 1860

BRINGUAN, Nicolas
Goldsmith: 1719

BRIZET, Jean
Goldsmith: 1776-1790

B. BROWER & CO.
(Baldwin Brower, George C. Brower, Elizabeth Barker Brower, later Mrs. William T.

Vanzandt, and William T. Vanzandt)
Crockery and House Furnishing Store: 1842-1855

S. & B. BROWER
(Samuel and Baldwin Brower)
House Furnishing Store: 1834-1842

BROWN, George C.
Silversmith: 1834-1835

BRUSSETIER, Benjamin
Jeweler and Goldsmith: 1816-1817

BUCKLEY, Henry Peat (1822-1903)
Jeweler:
1839-1842 (New York)
1842-1903 (New Orleans)
Successor of Young & Co., 1853

[BUNEL] Jacob
Goldsmith: 1763-1782
Slave of Jean-Baptiste Dominique Bunel. Freed in 1770s.

BUNEL, Jean-Baptiste Dominique (d. 1764)
Apprenticed in to Claude Dauvergne, Jr., usually of Mobile: 1738

CALDWELL, J. S.
Silversmith: 1843-1844

CAMP, William E. (1805-1874)
Watchmaker and Jeweler: 1832-1869

CAMP & DUBBS
(William E. Camp and Charles H. Dubbs)
Watchmaker, Silversmiths, and Jewelry Store: 1838

CANDIDE [AVINENC], August (1841-1871)
Jeweler: 1861-1871

CARIOLLE,
Silversmith: 1822-1823

CARRÉ, Jean (d. 1765)
Goldsmith

CASSARD, Edmond
Goldsmith: 1834-1835

CAVALLIER, Michel
Goldsmith: 1832

CAZENAVE,
Goldsmith: 1828

CHAMPAGNE, Thomas (b. 1796)
Silversmith: 1821

CHARPENTIER, J. F.
Goldsmith and Jeweler: 1852-1853

CHASSAGNE, Armand (b. 1786)
Goldsmith: 1820

CHASSAGNE, Thomas
Jeweler: 1822-1823

CHASTANT, Andre O.
Jeweler and Goldsmith: 1805-1827

CHEVREUIL, Guillaume (dit DUVAL) (d. 1726)
Goldsmith:
1707 (Quebec)
1725-1726 (New Orleans)

COCHRANE, William C.
Goldsmith: 1832

COMMOT, Pierre
Goldsmith: 1841-1842

COMTE, Pierre (b. 1693)
Goldsmith: 1719
Transported to Louisiana for tobacco smuggling.

CORBES, J.
Goldsmith: 1817

COUDRAIN, Pierre (1719/20 or 1729-1779)
Goldsmith and Jeweler: 1768-1779

COULON, Alexis
Goldsmith and Jeweler: 1853-1869

COURCELLE, Hilaire (1783-1852)
Goldsmith: 1822-1827

COUVERTIÉ, Emile (b. 1811)
Goldsmith and Jeweler: 1838-1867

COUVERTIÉ, Louis Gabriel (d. 1844)
Goldsmith:
1803(St. Marc, Santo Domingo)
1803-1809 (Santiago de Cuba)
1809-1815 (Baltimore)
1815-1844 (New Orleans)

DAGORRET, Jean
Goldsmith and Jeweler: 1830-1850

DANOU, Simon
Silversmith: 1849

DAPREMONT, Louis de la Lande
Merchant in partnership with James (Santiago) Fletcher: 1785-1790

DARBOIS, Louis
Goldsmith: 1830

DARTELLE, Gaston
Goldsmith: 1841-1842

DAUPHINE, Philip
Goldsmith: 1823

DAUVERGNE,
Goldsmith: 1822

DAUVERGNE, Claude
Master Goldsmith: 1732-1739

DELABORNE, Joseph
Goldsmith: 1832

DELAINE, Jean
Goldsmith: 1841-1842

DELARUE, Jean-Noel (1776-1842)
Goldsmith: 1802-1842
Partner of David Pentz, 1837-1842

DE MORSY, Jean
Goldsmith: 1811-1834

DESBAN, Michel
Goldsmith: 1811-1817

DEVINE, James (also DIVINE)
(d. 1842)
Jewelry Store: 1841-1842

DIEUDONNÉ, Francois (dit
FONDER) (d. 1738)
Founder, Jeweler, Goldsmith:
1725-1738

DILLON, Edward
Watchmaker, Jeweler, and Silversmith: 1852-1866
With Dillon & Hovel: 1856-1857

DILLON & HOVEL
(Edward Dillon & Hovel)
Watchmakers and Jewelers:
1856-1857

DOBBS, Henry M., Sr. (1765-1836)
Watchmaker: Prior to 1802-1804
(New York)
1805-1830 (New Orleans)

DOGI, Julien
Goldsmith: 1827

DOUTRE, St. Felix
Goldsmith: 1811

DRIVER, Major William C. (d.
1874)
Silversmith
With Hyde & Goodrich: 1861
With C. H. Zimmermann: 1866-1870

DROWN, Joseph
Watchmaker and Jeweler: 1838-1849

DROZ, Abraham
Watchmaker: 1763-1771

DUBIGNON, Jean (also DUBIGNEAU) (1779-1841)
Goldsmith: 1822-1838

DUBREUIL, Sebastian
Goldsmith: 1834-1835

DUCRET, Nicolas
Goldsmith: 1778

DUPRATEAU,
Goldsmith: 1817

DURCY, Ferdinand (1777-1851)
Silversmith: 1834-1835)

DUVAL See CHEVREUIL, Guillaume (dit DUVAL)

DUVERNET, F.
Goldsmith: 1778

EALER, Joseph E.
Silversmith: 1838-1842 (St. Louis)
Watchmaker: 1845-1870 (New Orleans)
With Gregor & Wilson: 1856
With C.H. Zimmermann & Co.:
1870

ENGLANDER,
Jeweler:
With Levi & Englander: 1865

EPPS, William
Jeweler and Watchmaker: 1866-1880
Successor to Louis Müh: 1866

ESTAN,
Goldsmith: 1813

FABER, Christian Friedrich (1814-1873)
Silversmith, Jeweler, and Diamond Setter: 1846-1873

FABER, William
Silversmith and Jeweler: 1868-1881

FAVRE, Justin
Goldsmith: 1842-1860
With Auguste Favre: 1849

FERRENBACH, Henry (1826-1854)
Watchmaker and Silversmith:
1850-1854

FERRIER, Jean
Goldsmith: 1816-1854

FEYTEL, Joseph
Jeweler, Watchmaker, and Silversmith: 1851-1870

FEYTEL & HUCHEZ
Watchmaker: 1838

FEYTEL & PERRET
(J. Feytel & A. Perret)
Watchmaker and Jewelry Store:
1841-1843

FILASSIER, Etienne (d. 1738)
Goldsmith: 1727-1738

FISCHALL,
Goldsmith: 1813

FITZGERALD,

FLETCHER, James (Santiago)
(d. 1809)
Apprenticed to Joseph Nixon,
silversmith, Dublin: 1771
Partnership with Louis Delalande Dapremont (merchant):
1787-1792

FORCHEIMER, S.
Goldsmith: 1851

FOUCHE, Louis
Silversmith: 1822

FOUCHER, Joseph
Goldsmith: 1827-1830

FRANTZ BROTHERS & CO.
(William and Henry Frantz,
George A. Hoffman, and Leopold Jansen)
Jewelers: 1898-1902

FRANTZ & OPITZ
(William Frantz and Henry
Opitz)
Jewelers: 1880-1897

WILLIAM FRANTZ & CO.
(William Frantz, George A. Hoffman, and Leopold Jansen)
Jewelers: 1903-1919

FRANTZ & SANDER
(William Frantz and A.H. Sander)
Manufacturing Jeweler and Diamond Setter: 1867

FRITZ, Henry (b. 1829)
Silversmith: 1860

GAINES & RELF
(John G. Gaines and Samuel Z.
Relf)
Crockery, Glass, and Silverware:
1865-1878

GAST, G. (b. 1820)
Jeweler and Galvanizer: 1868-1870

GERNON, William
Silversmith: 1843-1844

GEVROUIN, C.A.
Goldsmith: 1811

GIQUEL, Alexandre
Goldsmith: 1833-1835

GIQUEL, Jean-Baptiste Francois
(1777-1847)
Goldsmith and Jeweler: 1810-1832)

GIQUEL, J.B.T.
Goldsmith: 1834-1835

GISEAUME,
Goldsmith: 1811

GLON, Villeneuve
Goldsmith: 1846

GONTIER,
Goldsmith and Jeweler: 1838-1842

GOODRICH, Charles Whiting
(1780-1849)
Partner with James N. Hyde &
Co., New Orleans: 1819
Partner Hyde & Goodrich: after
1828

GRANDMAISON, Misse
Jeweler and Goldsmith: 1822-1827

GRAVIER, Nicholas (d. 1847)
Goldsmith and Spectacle Maker: 1797-1842

GREGOR, George W.
Jeweler: 1856-1861
With Gregor & Wilson: 1856-1858
With Gregor & Co.: 1858-1861

GREGOR & CO.
(George W. Gregor and R.L. Bruce)
Watchmaker and Jeweler: 1858-1861

GREGOR & WILSON
(George W. Gregor, John W. Gregor, and William A. Wilson)
Jewelers: 1856-1858

GRISWOLD, Arthur Breeze (1829-1877)
Partner, Hyde & Goodrich: from 1853
Partner, Thomas, Griswold & Co.
Partner, A.B. Griswold & Co.

A.B. GRISWOLD & CO.
Jewelry Store: 1865-1906
Successors to Thomas, Griswold & Co., and Hyde & Goodrich

A.B. GRISWOLD & CO., LTD.
Jewelers: 1906-1924
Bought out by Hausmann's, Inc.

GROS, Guillame (1751-1819)
Goldsmith: 1819

GUINAULT, Isaac or Ignace
Master Goldsmith: 1745-1766

GUYOMARS, James
Goldsmith: 1823 (New Orleans)
1837-1839 (Mobile)

HABAL, A.
Goldsmith: 1851

HABAL & CO.
(A. Habal)
Goldsmith: 1851

HAMMOND & PHILBRICK
(John T. Hammond and George Philbrick)
Watches, Jewelry, and Clocks: 1853-1854

HAMOT, William St. Leger (d. 1851) (free man of color)
Goldsmith and Jeweler: 1827-1844

HARLAND, Henry (1787-1841)
Silversmith and Watchmaker: 1805-1841 (Norwich, Connecticut)
1815-1832 (New Orleans)
Partner, Harland & Bliss: 1830

HARLAND & BLAIR
(Henry Harland and Daniel Blair)
Jewelers and Silversmiths: 1830-1834

HARLAND & BLISS
(Henry Harland and H. Bliss)
Jewelers: 1830

HARRIS, Frederick
Goldsmith and Silversmith: 1834-1835

HAUSMANN, Henry (1845-1878)
Jeweler and Silversmith: 1870-1880
With New Orleans Silver Manufactory: 1878
Successor to A. Himmel

HAUSMANN, Mrs. Henry (Theresa Rosenbuch) (1847-1924)
Jeweler: 1878-1924
With H. Hausmann: 1878-1880
Successor of H. Hausmann: 1881-1889

HAUSMANN, Theresa (1847-1924)
Jeweler: 1881-1889

T. HAUSMANN & SON
(Theresa Hausmann and Louis Hausmann)
Jewelers: 1890-1893

T. HAUSMANN & SONS
(Theresa Hausmann, Louis Hausmann, and Gabriel Hausmann)
Jewelers: 1894-1906

T. HAUSMANN & SONS, LTD.
Jewelers: 1906-1917

HAUSMANN'S, INC.
Jewelers: after 1918

HAZARD & BLAIR
(William Hazard and Daniel Blair)
Jewelry and Fancy Store: 1834

HEINRICH, Paul
Goldsmith and Jeweler
With J. Henry: 1870-1880

HENDERSON & GAINES
(William Henderson, Howard Henderson, John G. Gaines, Samuel Z. Relf)
Earthenware, China, and Crockery: 1841-1865

HENRY, Etienne Maximillian (b. 1798)
Goldsmith: 1821

HENRY, John
Watchcase Maker, Gold, and Silver Refiner and Assayer: 1867-1880

HERAUD,
Goldsmith: 1813

HERTZ, L.
Silversmith and Jeweler: 1855

HILL, Alvin M.
Gold Pen Manufactory and Jeweler: 1874-1909

HIMMEL, Adolphe (1825/6-1877)
Silversmith: 1852-1877
With Küchler & Himmel: 1852-1853
With Hyde & Goodrich: 1853-1861
With Thomas, Griswold & Co.: 1861-1865
With A.B. Griswold & Co.: 1865-1869
With A. Himmel Silverware Manufactory: 1869-1877

HOEFER, Theodore (b. 1852)
Goldsmith: 1870

HOERNER, Jules or Julius (see KELLER & HOERNER)

HOLYLAND, Frederick (d. 1894)
Engraver: 1865-1881

HOPKIS, Henry (b. 1801)
Silversmith: 1820

HUCHEZ (See FEYTEL & HUCHEZ)

HUFTY, Major Joseph (1806-1861)
Jewelry and Silverware

HUTCHINSON, William M. (d. 1832)
Silversmith: 1832

HYDE, James Nevins (1787-1838)
Jeweler: 1812-1818 (Partner in Hyde & Nevins, New York)
1818-1837 (Partner, James N. Hyde & Co., New York)
1816-1828 (Partner, James N. Hyde & Co., New Orleans)
1828-1837 (Partner, Hyde & Goodrich, New Orleans)

JAMES N. HYDE & CO.
Jewelry: 1818-1837 (New York)
1816-1828 (New Orleans)

HYDE & GOODRICH
(James Nevins Hyde, Charles Whiting Goodrich, Edward Goodrich Hyde, William McCleary Goodrich, Henry Thomas, Jr., Arthur Breeze Griswold)
Jewelry: 1828-1861

HYDE & NEVINS
1812-1818 (New York)

JACHAULT, Louis (Also JUCHAULT and SERCHAULT)
Goldsmith: 1817-1822

JACOB (Also BUNEL)
Goldsmith: 1763-1782
Slave of Jean Baptiste Dominique Bunel, freed in 1770s.

JACOBS, M.
Jeweler and Watchmaker: 1866-1867

JANSEN, August William (1835-1898)
Silversmith: 1870-1880
With C. Küchler & Co.: 1870

JEAN, Rene (b. 1667)
Goldsmith: 1719

JEBER, J
Goldsmith: 1778

JENNINGS, O.S.
Jeweler: 1860-1861

JOLLY, Pierre
Goldsmith and Watchmaker: 1745-1747

JOURDAIN, Samuel (Also JOURDAN S.)
Goldsmith: 1834-1835

JUCHAULT, Louis (Also JACHAULT and SERCHAULT)
Goldsmith: 1817-1822

KATZENSTEIN, Eugene (b. 1825)
Jeweler and Silversmith: 1852-1880

KELLER, T.A. (see KELLER & HOERNER)

KELLER & HOERNER
(T.A. Keller and Julius Hoerner)
Wholesale dealers and manufacturers of diamond jewelry and silverware: 1861-1865

KIDEL, Hubert
Goldsmith and Jeweler: 1826-1844

KING, Ernest
Goldsmith: 1854

KNOWLES & NOEL
Jewelers and Watchmakers: 1848-1850

KÜCHLER, Christopf Christian
Silversmith: 1852-1870
With Küchler & Himmel: 1852-1853
With Terfloth & Küchler: 1858-1866
With C. Küchler & Co.: 1870

C. KÜCHLER & CO.
(Christopf Christian Küchler and Augustus William Jansen)
Silversmith: 1870

KÜCHLER & HIMMEL
(Christopf Christian Küchler and Adolphe Himmel)
Silver Plate Workers: 1852-1853

KUNLER, Henry
Silversmith: 1861-1866

LEMANE, S.
Goldsmith: 1778

LAMBERT, Jean B.
Goldsmith: 1827-1830

LAMOTHE, (Jean-Marie and Jean-Baptiste)
Goldsmith and Engraver: 1824-1846

LAMOTHE, Pierre
Goldsmith and Jeweler:
Before 1803 (St. Marc, Santo Domingo)
1803-1809: (Santiago de Cuba)
1809-1823: (New Orleans)

LANDSEE, Xavier (1824-1870)
Silversmith, Watchmaker, and Jeweler: 1866-1870

LA PIERRE,
Jeweler: 1769

LA RIVE, Eustachio (b. c.1729)
(Also LORINE)
Silversmith: 1778-1789

LAWLER, William
Silversmith: 1842 (St. Louis)
1846-1855 (New Orleans)

LE DUF, Jacques
Goldsmith: 1811

LEVI, Isaac C.
Jeweler: 1880s

LEVI & ENGLANDER
Watches, Jewelry, and Silver: 1865-1868

LEZIAN, Francois
Goldsmith: 1824-1844

LEZIAN, Sanon
Goldsmith: 1822-1842

LILIENTHAL, Edward (1836-1888)
Watchmaker and Jeweler: 1858-1888

LILIENTHAL, Julius (1827-1867)
Jeweler and Watchmaker: 1853-1867

LINIBAUGH, James L.
Silversmith: 1830 (New Orleans)
(Memphis)

LOHMÜLLER, Sebastian (1822-1871)
Goldsmith: 1850-1871

LORINE, Eustache (See LA RIVE)

LUCAS, Jean
Goldsmith: 1811

LUIS,
Goldsmith: 1782

LUND & ANTZ
(N.H. Lund and George Antz)
Jewelers and Engravers: 1853-1855

MAGGEE, Thomas M. (b. 1828)
Silversmith: 1860

MAIROT, Jean-Claude (1774-1842)
Goldsmith: 1811-1835

MALLARD, Prudent (1809-1879)
Cabinetmaker, also importer of silverware: 1853-1857

MARCHAND, Evariste
Goldsmith: 1822-1842

MARCHAND, Louis
Goldsmith
With Simon & Louis Marchand: 1824

MARCHAND, Simon
Goldsmith
With Simon & Louis Marchand: 1824

MARSAC
Silversmith: 1833

MARTIN, J. M.
Silversmith: 1871

MCQUEREN, Edmund
Goldsmith: 1808

MEIGER, F
Goldsmith: 1844

MEILLEUR, Michel, Jr. (1818-1893)
Goldsmith and Jeweler: 1841-1846

MEILLEUR, [Jean-Baptiste] Theodore (1821-1864)
Goldsmith: 1846

MELVILLE & CO.
(David Melville)
Manufacturers of silver:
1849-1858 (New Orleans)
1852 (New York)

MEUNIER,
Goldsmith: 1837

MEYER, John C.
Jeweler and Goldsmith: 1860-1880s

MEYER, M.H. (1808-1887)
Watchmaker and Jeweler: 1841-1887

MICHEL, John E.
Watchmaker, Jeweler, and Goldsmith: 1829-1830

MICOUIN, Michel (b. 1695)
Goldsmith: 1719

MILLER, Gustave (See MÜLLER)

MILLER, Rudolphe (See MÜLLER)

MORGAN, William S.
Watchmaker and Jeweler:
1837-1846 (Poughkeepsie)
1846-1850 (New Orleans)

MORNET, Celestin
Goldsmith: 1841-1842

MÜH, Louis (1801-1882)
Watchmaker and Jeweler: 1822-1870
Succeeded by W.W. Rees & Co.: 1854
Succeeded by William Epps: 1866

MÜLLER, Gustave (b. 1825)
Goldsmith, Jeweler, and Watchmaker: 1858-1870

MÜLLER, Rudolphe
Silverworker: 1877-1930s

MYERS, Leon
Goldsmith: 1849-1859

NÉRESTAN, Adolphe
Silversmith: 1834-1835

NERO,
Goldsmith: 1818

NEWCOMBE, Calvin
Silversmith: 1817

NOEL, Washington
Jeweler
With Knowles & Noel: 1848-1850

OFFNER, E.
Crockery, China, and Silver Importer

OIGNAUD,
Goldsmith: 1818

OPITZ (See FRANTZ & OPITZ)

PACHE, Jean-Ignace (or Izaac) Olivier
Goldsmith: 1745-1746

PAULDING, Cornelius (d. 1851)
Merchant:
1801-1802 (New York)
1802-1810 (Savannah)
1810-1851 (New Orleans)

PECAULT,
Goldsmith: 1819

PENTZ, John David
Silversmith: 1837-1868
Partner of Jean-Noel Delarue: 1837-1842

PEPIN, Henry
Goldsmith:
1854 (New Orleans)
1858 (Bayou Sara, Louisiana)

PETERS, Frederick R. (b. 1827)
Silversmith: 1854-1874

PHILBRICK, George (see HAMMOND & PHILBRICK)

PHILLIPE, Joseph (1757-1831)
Jeweler and Goldsmith:
1796-1802 and 1819-1823 (Baltimore)
1810-1811 and 1825-1831 (New Orleans)

PINTA, Jean-Baptiste
Goldsmith: 1810-1819

POTTER, Alexander
Silversmith: 1849-1850

PRAAG, L. (see VON PRAAG)

PRATT, Sebastian (Also PRAT, PRATE)
Goldsmith: 1827-1835

PREVOST, Antoine (b. 1686)
Goldsmith:
1721-1736 (Fort St. Louis, Mobile)
1736-1766 (New Orleans)

PREVOST, Claude, Jr.
Goldsmith: 1747 (Mobile)

PRIOLLAUD, E.
Silversmith and Manufacturer: 1860-1870

PROESCHEL, Sigismond (1797-1833)
Goldsmith: 1830-1833

PROFILET, Emile (1801-1868)
Silversmith and Watchmaker:
1822 (New Orleans)
1823-1868 (Natchez, Mississippi)

RACICH, Nicholas
Jeweler: 1853-1870

RAFEL, Joseph (b. 1810)
Jeweler and Watchmaker:
New York
1842 (Cincinnati)
1852-1861 (New Orleans)

RAPHAEL, James
Goldsmith and Silversmith: 1832

RASCH, Anthony (1778/80-1858)
Goldsmith and Silversmith:
1794-1798 (Passau, Germany)
1801-1820 (Philadelphia)
1820-1858 (New Orleans)

REDON, Claudius (1788-1857)
Silversmith:
1828 (New York)
1830-1851 (New Orleans)

REES, William Windor (d. 1863)
Watchmaker and Jeweler: 1852-1861
Successor Louis Müh: 1854

RELF, Samuel Z. (see GAINES & RELF)

RENOIR, Alexander
Goldsmith, Engraver, and Jeweler: 1819-1832

REPONTIE, Auguste (Also REPONTY) (free man of color)
Goldsmith: 1822-1834

RICHET, C.
Jeweler and Silversmith: 1848-1851

RIVERA, P. Napoleon (c. 1820-1872)
Goldsmith and Jeweler: 1844-1871

ROBINSON & OLROYD
Silver Plate Workers: 1854-1856

ROCQUET, Leopold S. (1796-1851)
Goldsmith: 1827-1841
ROSS, Philip
Goldsmith: 1811-1838

ROUYER, Pierre Casimir
Goldsmith, Silversmith, Gilder, Plater, Galvanizer, and Medalist: 1850-1877
Successor to M. Lefebure: 1850

RYAN, James (b. 1838)
Silversmith: 1860

ST. CYR, S. L. (1795-1880)
Goldsmith and Jeweler: 1820-1860

ST. LEGER, William (See HAMOT)

SALM, Jacob
Watchmaker and Jeweler: 1851-1888

SALOMON, William (1822-1881)
Engraver and Goldsmith: 1841-1856
Apprenticed to John V. Childs, engraver: 1836

SALTZMANN, John Christian
Engraver: 1807-1834

SCHWANG, Jacob
Gold Beater: 1838

SCHNEIDER BROTHERS
(John and Nicholas Schneider)
Silversmiths, Piano factors, and Music Stores: 1842

SCHWALB, J. Philip (b. c. 1840)
Silversmith: 1860-1880

SCOOLER, Gabriel (b. 1835)
Jeweler and Watchmaker: 1857-1870

SCOOLER, Maurice (1827-1900)
Jeweler: 1842-1900

SEMPLE, Mathew (b. 1806)
Jeweler: 1851-1860

SERCHAULT (See JACHAULT and JUCHAULT)

SEVEIGNES, E. P.
Goldsmith and Jeweler: 1846-1858

SEVEIGNES, F
Goldsmith: 1842

SEVEIGNES, Jacques
Goldsmith: 1822-1837

SHEPARD, E. R.
Silversmith: 1866

SHIZMULLER, Frank (b. 1840)
Goldsmith: 1860

SIMEON, J. or S.
Goldsmith: 1810-1811

SIMONS, Leon
Jeweler: 1870-1880

SIMONIN, Dominique Leopold
(1818-1868)
  Manufacturing Jeweler: 1838-1868

SIMONT,
  Goldsmith: 1824

SNYDER, G. K.
  Silversmith: 1823-1830

SONGY, Francois (dit LA FRANCE)
  Founder, Goldsmith, and Merchant: 1720-after 1747

SONGY, Pierre
  Goldsmith: 1747-1771

STABLE,
  Goldsmith: 1811

STARKE, Henry (b. 1835)
  Silversmith: 1860

STICKNEY, Moses Peck (d. 1832)
  Silversmith and Watchmaker:
  1820 (Newberry, Massachusetts)
  1830-1832 (New Orleans)

STUBENRAUCH, F. (1815-1866)
  Jeweler and Hairworker: 1857-1866

TERFLOTH, Bernard (See TER-FLOTH & KÜCHLER)

TERFLOTH & KÜCHLER
  (Bernard Terfloth and C. Christian Küchler)
  Jeweler and Silversmith: 1858-1866

TESSIER, J. B. (b. 1796)
  Goldsmith: 1821

THEOFILE,
  Goldsmith: 1822

THOMAS, GRISWOLD & CO.
  (Henry Thomas, Jr., A. B. Griswold, William Goodrich, Henry Gindes, and A.L. Abbott)
  Jewelry Store: 1861-1865
  Successors of Hyde & Goodrich

THOMAS, Montplesaire
  Goldsmith: 1830

THOMAS, Richard
  Silversmith: 1807

THROOP, Orramel Hinckley
(b. 1798)

Silversmith and Engraver: 1831-1834

TOULASSE,
  Goldsmith and Watchmaker:
  1818-1820

TOUSSAINT, Auguste (b. c. 1796)
  Goldsmith and Watchmaker:
  1819-1830

TREMELLS, Robert
  Goldsmith: 1811

TREVIGNE, Eugene
  Goldsmith: 1830

TURK, Mrs. Susan (Widow of Joseph)
  Watchmaker and Jeweler: 1856-1860

TURPIA, Jacques (b. 1812)
  Goldsmith and Jeweler: 1842-1855

TURPIN & CO.
  Goldsmith: 1811

TYLER, Edward A. (1815-1879)
  Silversmith and Jeweler:
  1834-1838 (Belfast, Maine)
  1838-1879 (New Orleans)

VALLEE, Antoine
  Goldsmith, Watchmaker, and Engraver: 1810-1822

VIGNAUD, Jean L.
  Watchmaker and Dry Goods:
  1816-1830

VILLE, Bazile
  Goldsmith: 1822-1835
  Partner in Ville & Belliard: 1822

VILLE & BELLIARD
  (Bazile Ville and Francois Belliard)
  Goldsmith: 1822-1823

VILLIO, Joseph J. (Also VILLOT, VILLIOD, VILLIOT) (c. 1822-1889)
  Jeweler, Goldsmith, and Diamond Setter: 1856-1859

VITAUT, Jacques
  Goldsmith and Jeweler: 1830-1834

von PRAAG, L.
  Silversmith: 1859

WEST, J.
  Jeweler and Goldsmith: 1846

WHITTEMORE, Edwin (1798-1867)
  Jeweler and Watchmaker:
  1830-1833 (Natchez, Mississippi)
  1833-1867 (New Orleans)
  With Coit & Whittemore, Natchez, Mississippi: 1830-1833
  With Bliss & Whittemore, New Orleans: 1833-1835
  With Whittemore & Blair, New Orleans: 1838-1840
  With Whittemore & Young, New Orleans: 1841

WHITTEMORE & BLAIR
  (Edwin Whittemore and Daniel Blair)
  Jeweler: 1838-1840

WHITTEMORE & YOUNG
  (Edwin Whittemore & Nelson A. Young)
  Jeweler: 1841

WILSON, William A. (b. 1831)
  Watchmaker and Jeweler: 1856-1861
  With Gregor & Wilson: 1856-1858

WODOM, Miguel
  Silversmith: 1788-1790

YOUNG, James A.
  Watchmaker: 1842

YOUNG, Nelson A.
  Watchmaker and Jeweler: 1841-1850
  With Whittemore & Young: 1841
  Succeeded by Young & Co.: 1850

YOUNG & CO.
  (Mrs. Nelson A. Young and H. P. Buckley)
  Jewelry Store: 1850-1853

YSABELLE, P. J. (Also ISABEL)
  Jeweler and Goldsmith: 1831-1832

ZIMMERMANN, Charles H.
  Jeweler and Silversmith: 1866-1870

ZIMMERMANN, P.
  Silversmith and Jeweler: 1865

The following list, assembled by the authors, is a compilation of marks used by New Orleans silversmiths during the nineteenth and early twentieth centuries. This list represents most marks on New Orleans silver found to date by the authors. It is hoped that the publication of this list will encourage more research in the area of identifying marks. The primary purpose of illustrating them is to aid owners of New Orleans-made silver in the identification of their holdings.

The name of each silversmith or firm is followed by an illustration of the maker's mark. In some instances, more than one mark is pictured, to show variations and wholesale changes in the look of the mark throughout an individual's or firm's period of activity. The small number beside each mark denotes the museum or collection which owned the piece providing the illustration. The numerical designations represent the following sources:

1. Anglo-American Art Museum
2. The Henry Francis duPont Winterthur Museum
3. The Historic New Orleans Collection
4. The Missouri Historical Society
5. Yale University Art Gallery
6. Private Collection

ADAM, Hilaire ... 6

B (unattributed mark) ... 6

H.E. BALDWIN & CO. ... 6 ... 1

BELLANGER, Jean P. ... 6

BERTIN, Pierre ... 1

BIRTEL, Frank G. ... 6

BLISS & WHITTEMORE ... 6

BONNET, Adrien ... 6

BOUJOU, Joseph ... 4

B. BROWER & CO. ... 6

S. & B. BROWER ... 6

BUCKLEY, Henry Peat ... 3

COUVERTIÉ, Louis ... 6

DELARUE, Jean-Noel ... 6 ... 6 ... 6

DROWN, Joseph ... 6

FEYTEL, Joseph N. ... 6

FITZGERALD ... 6

FRANTZ BROTHERS & CO. ... 6

GIQUEL, Jean - Baptiste Francois ... 6

GREGOR & WILSON ... 6

A. B. GRISWOLD & CO. ... 1

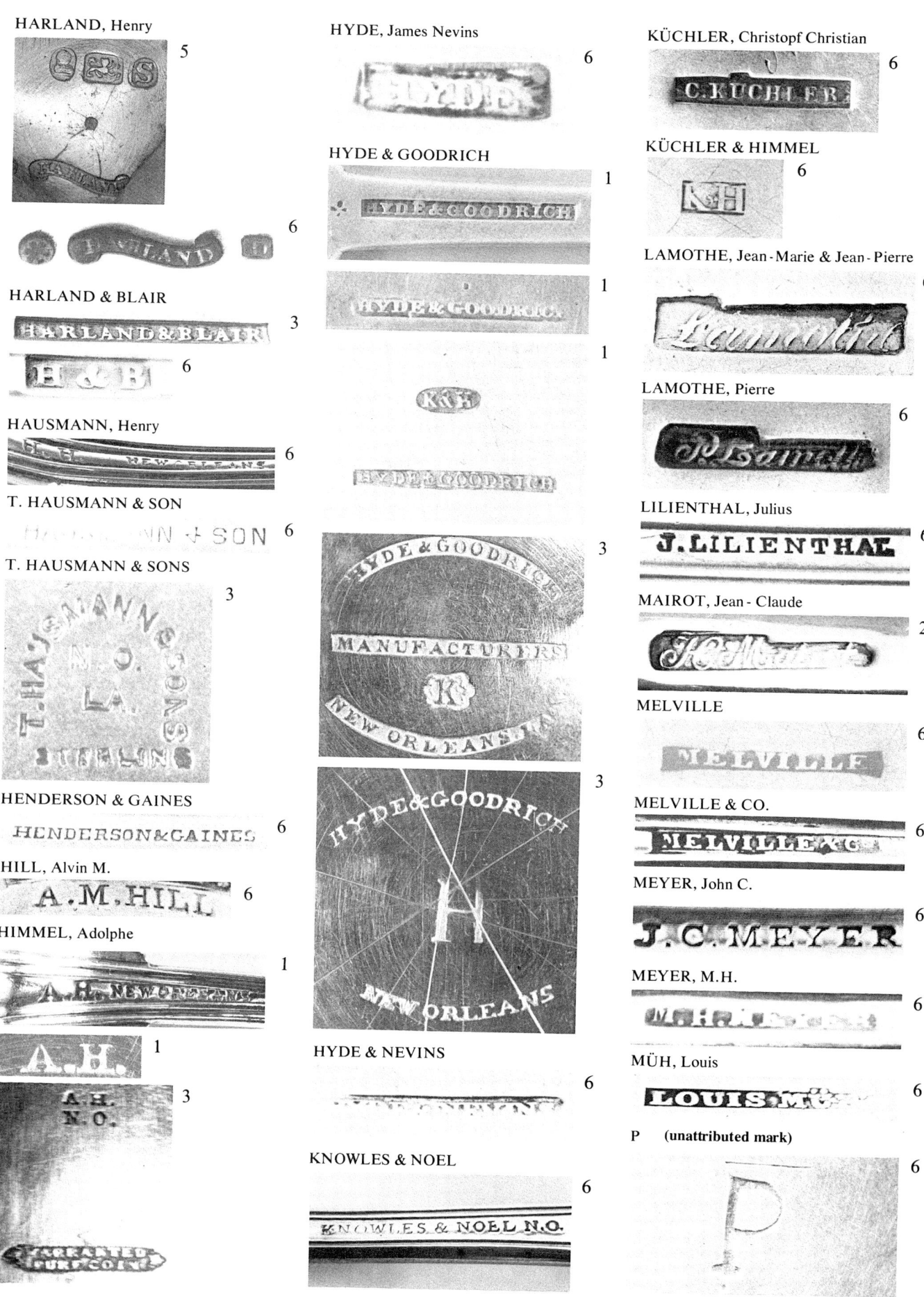

HARLAND, Henry   5

HARLAND   6

HARLAND & BLAIR   3

   6

HAUSMANN, Henry   6

T. HAUSMANN & SON   6

T. HAUSMANN & SONS   3

HENDERSON & GAINES   6

HILL, Alvin M.   6

HIMMEL, Adolphe   1

   1

   3

HYDE, James Nevins   6

HYDE & GOODRICH   1

   1

   1

   3

   3

HYDE & NEVINS   6

KNOWLES & NOEL   6

KÜCHLER, Christopf Christian   6

KÜCHLER & HIMMEL   6

LAMOTHE, Jean-Marie & Jean-Pierre   6

LAMOTHE, Pierre   6

LILIENTHAL, Julius   6

MAIROT, Jean-Claude   2

MELVILLE   6

MELVILLE & CO.   6

MEYER, John C.   6

MEYER, M.H.   6

MÜH, Louis   6

P   (unattributed mark)   6

RAFEL, Joseph

3

J.RAFEL·N·O

6

J. RAFEL

RASCH, Anthony

6

A·RASCH   N·ORLEANS

6

A RASCH

REDON, Claudius

6

C·REDON

W.W. REES & CO.

6

W.W. REES & CO

ROCQUET, Leopold S.

6

ROUYER, Pierre Casimir

6

C·ROUYER

SCOOLER, Gabriel

6

G.SCOOLER

SCOOLER, Maurice

6

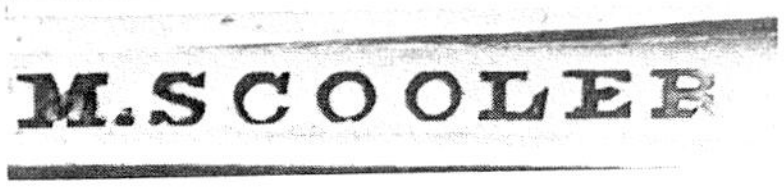

M.SCOOLER·N·O

6

M.SCOOLER

SIMONS, Leon

2

L.SIMONS

TERFLOTH & KÜCHLER

6

TERFLOTH & KUECHLER
N. ORLEANS. LA.

TURK, Susan

6

S.TURK

TYLER, Edward A.

6

E.A.TYLER·N·ORLEANS

E.A.TYLER.

1

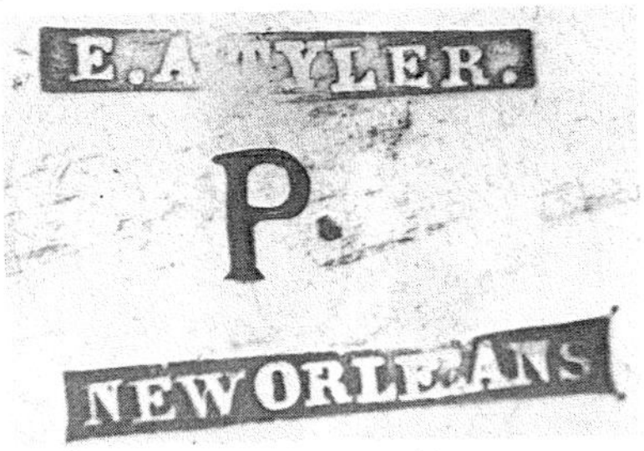

NEW ORLEANS

E.A.TYLER.

6

P.

NEW ORLEANS

V,I.   (unattributed mark)

6

LV

WHITTEMORE & BLAIR   -

1

WHITTEMORE & BLAIR

YOUNG & CO.

6

YOUNG & CO

ZIMMERMANN, Charles H.

1

C.H.ZIMMERMANN

ZIMMERMANN, P.

6

P. ZIMMERMANN

PHOTOGRAPH CREDITS

CRESCENT CITY
SILVER

THE HISTORIC NEW ORLEANS COLLECTION

Stanton Frazar, Director
Dode Platou, Chief Curator
John A. Mahé II, Curator
Rosanne McCaffrey, Associate Curator
John H. Lawrence, Assistant Curator
Lisette C. Oser, Registrar
Tom Staples, Preparator

Auseklis Ozols, Design Consultant

ANGLO-AMERICAN ART MUSEUM

H. Parrott Bacot, Curator